AF290762

Julie von Bismarck

Connections in the horse

Publisher's imprint

Julie von Bismarck
Connections in the horse
ISBN: 978-3-9822821-4-5
Originally published in German as
"*Zusammenhänge im Pferd*" ISBN: 978-3-9820414-1-4
Copyright Julie von Bismarck
3rd edition, paperback published 2019
English translation: Sue Anderson for
Anima Translation
Printer: BoD
Self-published by Verlag von Bismarck
Julie von Bismarck
Herrenholz 18
23556 Lübeck
Germany
Illustrations: private; photographs: private and istock photo
This work, including all parts hereof, is protected by copyright.
Any use outside the narrow limits of copyright law is prohibited
unless with the author's consent. This applies in particular to any
electronic or other form of reproduction, translation, distribution
or public dissemination.
Printed in Germany

Contents

Foreword

In the twenty-plus years in which I have treated a wide variety of horses in countries all over the world, a number of connections have become clear to me – connections I wouldn't even have dreamed of before.

Even as a child, I had always been struck by unusual behaviour in horses grazing at pasture, carrying riders or pulling a carriage, and as I learned to ride better, I became aware of more connections between humans and horse welfare. But I hadn't expected to find such complexity in the connections between seemingly small triggers and serious physical consequences for the horse.

If I'd known sooner how a heavy hand on the rein or the sting of a spur can affect the horse's welfare, I'd have been much more careful about the way I rode and handled horses than I already was due to the strict rules in our family.

I am firmly convinced that most of the riders and owners whose horses I have "repaired" over the years would have felt the same way.

This includes a rather sobering realisation: the vast majority of the blockages I have treated – the mental and physical damage and impairments, as well as chronic conditions – could have been prevented.

With a little more knowledge about the horse and the art of riding, certain mistakes could have been avoided.

Knowing about some of these connections – between physical blockages, injuries and diseases of the horse, and also between riding and handling styles and the resulting, sometimes hugely adverse effects on the horse's well-being – will help you to see your horse with different eyes.

As in my first book and other publications, I aim in this book to make a difference to horse welfare by sharing my observations and experience.

I remain convinced that knowledge and education are the best tools we have to return to a style of riding that places the horse's welfare at the centre of attention and the responsibility squarely on the rider.

NB: The contents of this book are derived solely from my personal experience and observations, and are not intended as a scientific treatise. For ease of understanding, the information has been kept short and simple, and so is deliberately not explained in its full complexity.

Chapter 1

Shifting baselines in equestrian sport and the consequences for horse welfare

When I was learning to ride, "being a rider" was a mark of distinction that came with following some extraordinarily strict rules, values and traditions.

In a nutshell, these rules made the horse's welfare the top priority and placed the responsibility on the shoulders of the rider.

Acting ethically towards the horse came naturally as a result of adhering to these rules and values, the first of which was: the fault never lies with the horse.

Either the rider has done something wrong – misjudged a situation or given unclear aids – or the rider has overworked the horse, i.e. asked it to do something it wasn't capable of doing. Mentally or physically.

Anyone who wants to ride must first have the physical fitness, ability and self-discipline to achieve the intended performance in the saddle, regardless of how much the horse has already learned or is able to do.

Anyone wanting to be a rider must therefore take full responsibility for the mental and physical well-being of their horse before they're even allowed into the saddle.

This basic rule was never broken. But today, unfortunately, this is no longer the case in many places. The basic rules have shifted. Shifting baselines.
Shifting baseline syndrome is part of human nature: people get accustomed to the strangest of things, which slowly but surely become the new reality. This is the case in every area of society. In equestrian sport, sadly, the consequences for the horse can be fatal.

So let's take a quick look at the trends that ultimately led to this shift in basic principles.

"Equestrianism" used to be a pretty exclusive club, for the simple reason that riding – with all the training, tack and equipment it entails, and not forgetting the horses – cost an awful lot of money. Equestrianism was known as a good way to burn cash, but not as a way to earn money or indeed to add to an existing pool of wealth.
This applied to riding instructors, whose job encompassed responsibility for the stables, including the care of the horses, and to saddlers, who not only upholstered the saddles of high society but also its sofas and armchairs, and also to blacksmiths, who not only shod the horses but also made the wrought-iron gates and fences of the estates where the animals grazed.

But when "equestrianism" became the mass participation sport of "horse riding", all of this suddenly changed.

Riding suddenly went from a national necessity (mounted cavalry) or an expensive hobby (see above) to an industry in its own right, something you could earn a crust from, or even a decent living. Suddenly there were masses of people who wanted to ride, and of course they all needed horses and farriers and instructors and saddlers; suddenly there were blacksmiths, instructors and saddlers who only shod horses, only taught riders and only upholstered saddles – as their full-time jobs.

Breeders too, of course, saw their sales increase and new occupations sprang up in the niches of this trend. People, for example, who made their living solely from training and selling horses.

None of this was necessarily a bad thing, it's just that this rush to ride suddenly made the existing complexities of rider and horse training too time-consuming.

Training was too difficult and/or too strenuous for the prospective riders and too expensive for the horse sellers, who by now were mostly identical with the trainers.

The sooner you could get a horse into competition, the sooner you could use it to make money.

The sooner a horse mastered its exercises or jumped impressive heights, the sooner it could be sold and the higher the price.

The sooner you could rack up "successes" for a satisfied student, the more new students would come knocking on your door, which in turn meant: more money.

The numbers of people who just wanted to ride because they'd always dreamed of sitting on a horse kept growing.

More and more people took up the opportunity of "learning to ride" without incurring any major personal commitment or financial expense.

That's all very well.

The horse, however, is a complicated creature and learning to ride is a very complex process. It takes years and vast amounts of training to develop a reasonably good, well-balanced, independent seat.

And it usually takes just as long to develop the fast responses, self-control and intimate knowledge of the horse's nature that constitute the foundations for riding and handling a horse in a way that keeps it healthy and comfortable.

For this reason alone, a rider's training cannot be simplified and this "flattening out" of training, which superficially seems to work, was one of the major steps towards a sport that takes place at the expense of horse welfare.

The other major step was the radical shortening of the horse's training. This used to continue until horses were seven or eight years old; now they have to take part in competitions at the tender age of three. An age when they are still in the middle of growing and are literally nowhere near to being fully developed adults, either mentally or physically.

Today's three-year-old horses are asked to piaffe and to jump heights over 1m 25, just to see if the "disposition" is there. As if breeding showy movements is any substitute for years of basic training and strengthening. The focus is solely on performance: the goal is to have a horse that is as ready as possible as soon as possible.
However, the basic schooling of the horse – comprising many years of carefully thought-out physical and mental strengthening and exercising – is the only thing that can prevent a horse from becoming damaged by riding.

This dropping of the rule that a horse is considered "green" until the age of seven or eight, and that work during this time is confined to muscle strengthening and confidence building, was the second major step towards a sport at the expense of horse welfare. Despite all the information and knowledge available, and as the worst possible action in terms of ethics.
Had the old guidelines and principles been followed, it would have been impossible to simplify the rider's training or shorten the horse's schooling.
But the training manuals so carefully devised by the old riding masters and equestrian experts were unceremoniously relegated to the back of a drawer by the "new" riding instructors, trainers and sellers. Out of sight, out of mind.

Almost as soon as the drawers had closed, this knowledge of genuine, original horsemanship was summarily replaced by things that no longer had anything to do with the goal of keeping the horse healthy. What they did do was to allow anyone to compete successfully on suitably highly bred and talented horses within the space of a year.
Or to parade proudly in front of the mirrors in their local riding school on a swan-necked horse, or to career around the round pen and forests on a horse with a hollow back and nose sticking up in the air...

Horses were increasingly downgraded to "things" that were purely about usability, reliability in lessons and jumping ability.

Knowledge of the horse, its instincts, its finely tuned senses, its physicality, was passed on only to a limited extent, namely "the horse's tendency is to run", which was why the first priority had to be maintaining control.

And since this can be prevented in the original riderly sense only with patience, diligence, cleverness and discipline, an approach that would have required time, money and personal commitment from the riders, the horse was quickly reduced to a thing that anyone can steer and control using certain "tools":

Years of disciplined theoretical and practical training were now replaced by simply giving riders rope halters, draw-reins, sharp bridles and coercive methods such as "Rollkur/LDR" (forced over-flexion/Low, Deep and Round) as a completely transparent substitute for riding skill and ability and conscientious basic schooling of rider and horse. Riders kitted themselves out with saddle-gripping jodhpurs moulded to their rears and saddles that automatically held the leg in position – and suddenly these, and the rhinestone-studded boots and bridles, were more important than the actual schooling.

The original meaning of equestrianism, its actual core values, was increasingly overlaid by tools and tricks to compensate for lack of training.
The trainers could boast satisfied customers, puffing out their chests in pride as they cleared impressive jumps or "rode" the highest-level dressage lessons on their coerced, stressed, overworked horses to cries of "Great ride!" And the horses suffered the consequences.
They still do so today, because sadly this style of riding has become the norm in recent decades. Shifting baselines at the expense of horse welfare.

It is the horses who suffer under an unbalanced seat, clumsy hands tugging on a sharp bit, draw-reins pulling their heads down to their chests, spurs digging into their sensitive skin at every step.
It is the horses who, because they haven't been diligently prepared for the tasks, suffer from permanent stress, pain and overwork, whose joints and muscles wear out and who are then simply replaced when they are "broken".

Fortunately, these behaviours and teaching methods are not ubiquitous, but for decades now most riders have learned to ride in this way or similar ways and consider it normal for horses to suffer from back pain or sore polls or arthritis.

Classic shifting baseline syndrome: through decades of teaching false principles, they slowly but surely became the reality

It used to be generally accepted that it takes around seven to eight years to train a horse and at least as long to actually learn to ride, but today it is considered normal for three-year-olds to look, behave and perform like adult horses.
It is considered normal for riders to resort to "tools" that can be used to coerce the horse when communicating with it doesn't work due to a lack of knowledge or training.
The "horseman" reaches for the painful rope halter and sharp curb bit, the average rider for the "stud chain" and draw-reins.
It is considered normal for horses to be casually subjected to abhorrent methods such as Rollkur/LDR. The FEI (International Federation for Equestrian Sports) even describes this brutal kind of treatment as a "technique and training method".

The fact that riders who act in these ways then go on to win world championships and other major competitions exacerbates this "new normal", making it something worth striving for, so it finds many imitators.

So no-one is surprised any more when exercises to test the careful schooling of rider and horse are dropped from the hardest dressage tests because riders can no longer complete them.

Similarly, it is considered normal when obstacles devised to test the same parameters are redesigned and "dumbed down" because bad riders keep coming to grief on horses that are far too young and completely overtaxed (because they haven't been properly schooled).

This, of course, paints a picture that is terribly hard to neutralise (Figs. 1–9).

Which is precisely why we should all consider the issue of ethics in equestrian sport: it is not about a snapshot from the past, but a situation that persists to this day in much of the riding world. And this situation has massive health consequences for the horses.

Consequences that, as we will see in the course of this book, extend far beyond conditions of the joints, muscles and bones.

Fig. 1: Chains and ropes instead of trust and partnership.

Fig. 2: Use of draw-reins: tack as a substitute for training.

Fig. 3: Horse put into fight or flight mode by inflicting pain. Fly ears and padding under the noseband, which is cinched much too tightly, are no substitute for riding ability. Riders in the past weren't given a curb bit until they could ride well enough not to need it. Nowadays, riders use curb bits because they can't control their horse on a snaffle, and tight curb reins are regarded as normal.

To get an idea of how other people perceive equestrian sport today, I asked around a hundred riders and non-riders what sort of associations first come to mind when they hear the word "riding".
The non-riders frequently mentioned childhood characters such as "Wendy" or "Hanni and Nanni", but even more common were phrases such as "animal cruelty" and "hobby at the horse's expense". The riders' responses were dominated by associations such as "harmony", "partnership" and "love for the horse".

I was curious to see if and how the answers would change, so I then asked the same interviewees what sprang to mind in response to the combination "riding and ethics".

The non-riders stuck with "animal cruelty" as their most common association, followed by phrases such as:
"riders' dogged, aggressive faces"
"stressed, scared horses"
"overweight people on tortured-looking horses"

The riders' results were surprising. Simply adding "ethics" changed the associations significantly:
"loss of value"
"greed/profit"
"showy steps, rigid backs and unnatural movements"
"too much too soon"
"blood rule"
"Rollkur/LDR"
"coercion and violence"

"false ambition"
"poor training"

Two things are worth noting here:

First: the riders in my survey had only positive associations with the term "riding", but at the same time they seemed fully aware that little progress has been made in equestrian sport in terms of ethics.

Second: neither the riders nor the non-riders mentioned the concepts that I myself associate with riding: full responsibility for the horse and the duty to put the horse's welfare first at all times. This applies to keeping, handling and every style of riding.
Instead, it appears that anyone hearing the combination "ethics and riding" today immediately conjures up visions of horses forced into unnatural postures with their noses pulled down to their chests, desperately rolling their eyes forward in an attempt to widen their field of vision, or indeed to see anything at all.

Horses with their mouths tied closed, coerced into unnatural postures by force and sharp bridles, made to perform in ways that these postures make biomechanically impossible.
Poorly trained riders competing over demanding jumps while using the most painful types of bridle on horses trained carelessly, far too young and far too fast. Horses that are often shown only in canter

and walk because they are lame in trot, as any lay person could see.

Clenched-up Western horses, whose hindquarters and back muscles have barely scraped through azoturia ("tying up") before they are being grimly and relentlessly driven from one "sliding stop" to the next by the cowboys on their backs, aided by a long-shanked curb bit and even longer jagged spurs.

"Leisure riders" who "pursue their hobby" on badly muscled horses without any proper schooling and without any physical fitness of their own.

Fig. 4: Use of a twisted wire bit to exert the strongest possible effect on the horse's sensitive lower jaw. At this point the bone is covered only by mucous membrane and gum; the pain inflicted by this type of bit makes it very easy to pull the horse's mouth down to its chest for control.

Fig. 5: Poorly trained rider who pulls the bit through the horse's mouth and has spurs on her boots. In the past, you literally had to earn your spurs. Today, they are regarded as basic kit for every beginner. Here again, there seems to be an assumption that tack and equipment can substitute for training.

Fig. 6: Sliding stop achieved using a Western curb bit rather than finely tuned coordination and weight aids.

Fig. 7: Lack of riding ability with a seat that is so unbalanced that even bending forward slightly to praise the horse causes it to be stabbed in the belly by the long rowelled spurs.
One reason why riders in the past weren't given spurs until they could ride well enough not to need them.

Based on my experience and encounters with horses, riders and owners all over the world, with patients ranging from "leisure horses" to competitors in major international tournaments, I would divide equestrian sport as it exists today into two main groups in terms of ethics:

The first group clearly includes all of those riders who, despite knowing better and being able to judge the consequences of their actions, deliberately choose to ignore this knowledge.

For example, riders who don't keep their horses in horse-friendly ways, deciding that an hour's exercise in the horse walker will do, rather than letting them run free on grass all day.

Riders who fuel their horses on fancy feeds, using high stress levels and bags of excess energy as a substitute for years of meticulous schooling and strengthening.

Riders who know that there is no substitute for this schooling and that to do without it is detrimental to the horse's health.

Riders who then resort to extravagant, uncomfortable tack in order to keep these machines (which they deliberately made "hot" and "haywire") under any sort of control, and in this way drive their horses through the toughest of courses and dressage tests.

This group includes those riders who, rather than spending years training their horses with trust, patience and wisdom, simply force them to submit (by the way, it doesn't matter for how long: a few seconds are enough to do lasting damage) with coercion and compulsion, Rollkur, LDR or however else they want to describe the constricting of horses' necks.

This includes the FEI (International Federation for Equestrian Sports), which has declared these methods to be recognised "training methods" and specifically permits them: "The technique known as Low, Deep and Round (LDR), which achieves flexion without undue force, is acceptable." *

At this point I'd like to say a bit more for clarity.

The FEI says of itself: "Our values at the very heart of our endeavours: Horse First: The welfare of the horse is our top priority."**

If the FEI´s top priority really is "the welfare of the horse", they should not be permitting the "technique" LDR. Period.

"…which achieves flexion without undue force" really is a cynical wording - especially if you look at how those riders use the curb in dressage (and other painful bits in show jumping).

This wording is so grotesque that we must unfortunately assume that the FEI has somehow still not understood the massive suffering that "riding" in Rollkur/LDR entails for a horse.

More about this in later chapters, but on the specific topic of Rollkur, LDR, hyperflexion, unnatural postures, etc., I will say this now:

*https://inside.fei.org/news/fei-round-table-conference-resolves-rollkur-controversy
**https://inside.fei.org/fei/about-fei/values

It is wholly irrelevant whether a horse is "ridden" in such a posture for two minutes or ten. These actions can cause damage and stress to a horse within the space of a few seconds.
Why?
The "rider" brings the horse into a completely unnatural posture in which not only his natural movements are impaired. Its breathing is obstructed, its field of vision is massively restricted and pain is inflicted by the hyperflexion.
If loud music, spectators, flags, etc. haven't already done so, this triggers an automatic, evolutionary biological response known as the fight or flight instinct (see Chapter 3), which in very simplified terms means that:

The muscles are put under enormous tension, the head is carried as high as possible in order to locate the danger, stress hormones are released, the immune system is suppressed, the blood supply to "unimportant" organs such as the skin or digestive system is reduced in favour of the muscles, and the brain reverts to reptilian level (so the horse doesn't think about whether to escape the danger to the left or right, but simply runs) – by the way, not the best preconditions for expecting a horse to cope with tricky exercises or technically demanding jumps.
And this state is maintained until the danger has passed. Now it is conceivable (to put it cautiously) that with some riders the danger never does pass for the horse, and that the many stomach ulcers, respiratory conditions and fungal skin infections

found in horses "ridden" in this way, as well as the "behavioural abnormalities" such as weaving, crib-biting and self-mutilation, do not happen by chance. But after competing or enduring this sort of "training", even if these horses were to return to a quiet, peaceful home with all-day grazing on sunny, fragrant meadows, with easy-going carers and riders and gentle, thoughtful, horse-friendly training, that one moment in which the horse tries to obey his impulse and lift his head to expand his field of vision – and cannot, due to the forced posture – is enough to cause him harm.

Even in that one moment, blockages kick in and affect the entire cervical spine, the joints in the head and the transition between neck and shoulder.

These blockages are enough to cause lameness in all four legs, inflammation in the back, diseases of the organs and chronic pain.

But simply the stress of not being able to lift its head and look around is a form of animal cruelty.

The shortness of breath caused by the sore larynx, which incidentally also makes it hard to swallow saliva, the horse's only buffer against its stomach acid, adds to this stress, as does the pain in the joints and muscles of the head and neck.

Pressure in the poll and tightness in the throat, the two sites a predator would attack in order to bring down and kill the horse, transport it in evolutionary terms to a place where it fears for its life, not a place of suppleness and loose impulsion over its back.

Something that used to be regarded as the basis of

all dressage riding and without which you wouldn't have won a single competition.

Today, apparently, it is no longer considered necessary, as we now have these new "training methods and techniques".

The FEI should be aware that, while people may have succeeded in breeding horses with even more spectacular movements and apparently an enormous capacity for suffering, the horse's instincts have remained the same.

The horse is one of the most sensitive creatures on earth. To make it submit through force and coercion is not only completely unnecessary, but also has exceptionally severe consequences for the horse's well-being.

Inflicting pain and stress on horses in this way is a clear violation of animal welfare legislation, and to describe it as a "training method" or "technique" is therefore unparalleled in its cynicism.

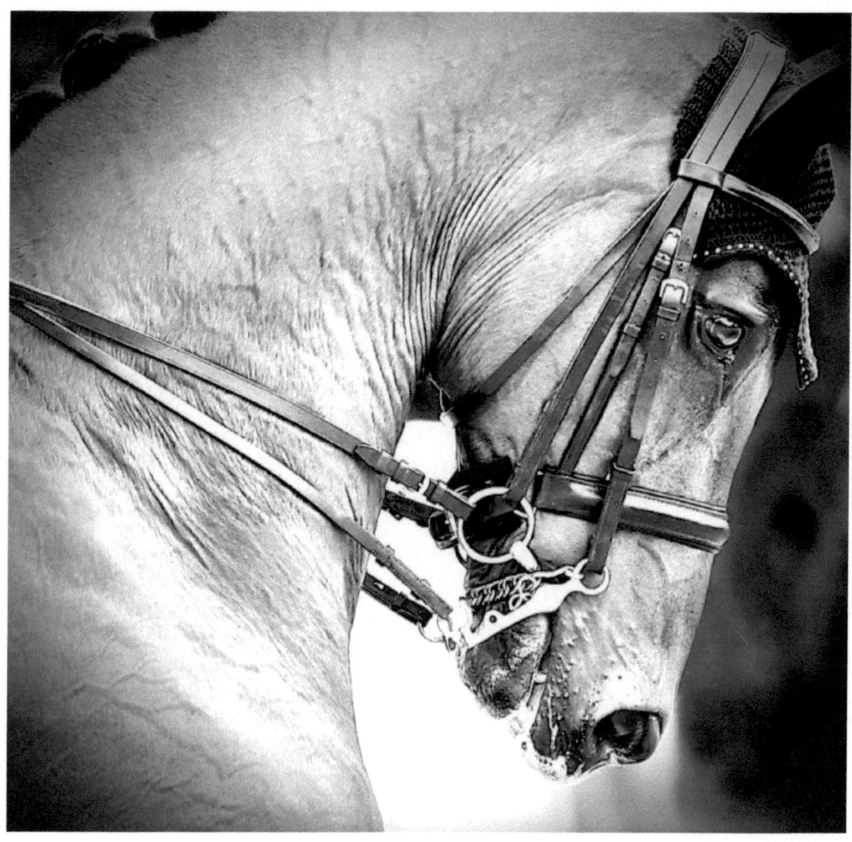

Fig. 8: "Low Deep and Round = LDR" in dressage. In this case the head is pulled higher up on the neck and chest than in other known images. Tightly cinched noseband, thin bradoon bit pulled through the mouth, fixed chin chain and a curb rein under high tension. The exact opposite of what was originally meant by the "art of dressage".
Shifting baselines.

Fig. 9: "LDR" = Rollkur in show jumping, here again with twisted wire as a "bit". Control through the use of painful tack and coercion.

Going back to my "ethics" classification, this first group also includes all of those riders who try to compensate for their own poor riding skills and a lack of carefully designed schooling for their horses by using sharp bridles, coercion and force.
This group includes any rider who lacks the necessary self-discipline for riding and takes their aggression out on the horse.

It also includes those riders who have a horse in pain "injected fit" or (to avoid doping detection, because "acupuncture can't be detected in the blood...") try to compel their "quack acupuncturist", all of a sudden no longer a quack, into giving their horses pain-suppressing acupuncture before a competition or auction.
These riders of course know very well that acupuncture is banned in competition, just like pain suppressors and many other drugs, and that injecting a sick horse "fit" rather than providing appropriate, consistent treatment is also an animal welfare issue.
(Yes, this too happens on a daily basis and I've had quite a few "requests" like these.)

In short: this group includes all of those riders who do their horses harm despite knowing better.

The second "ethics" group includes all of those riders who harm their horses not deliberately, but because they lack the necessary knowledge.

There are some riders for whom riding is a way to relax and restore balance, and often a form of personal development, who don't want to go to the effort of rider training in the original sense and think their knowledge of horses is sufficient. They want riding to be fun and don't want it to turn into work. Rather than investing in their own training, these riders often prefer to invest in a saddle that is touted on the internet as being especially "gentle on the horse's back" plus is so comfortable for the rider that it compensates for any lack of riding ability. Going to the special lengths of buying a "back-friendly" saddle for their horse makes them feel they have acted "pro-horse", and their consciences are clear as they ride around arenas and countryside with a thumping seat and restless hands on the hollowed back of a horse tensed up in pain.

The resulting back pain and blockages in the horse are often dismissed with comments such as: "He can't have anything wrong with him, after all I ride him with the special back-saving healthy saddle."

Rather than spending on the vet, osteopath or riding instructor, they then often invest in matching bandages and saddle pads and rugs and ear bonnet all in the genuine conviction that they are doing "everything for the horse".

Unfortunately, however, fancy kit is no substitute for training and the horse doesn't care if the saddle pad matches your breeches. What he needs is a balanced, safe, well trained rider and someone to cure his back pain.

However, this second group also includes those riders who do in fact do everything for their horse, for whom their horse's well-being is indeed the primary concern.

These are the riders who call the osteopath or vet every time their horse cocks an ear, who attend weekend seminars and lectures on horse health and good riding, and fill bowls with carrots, apples and alfalfa, and wash and oil hooves every day.

These riders try their very best to do everything right and would literally give their horse the shirt off their backs.

So it's especially deplorable if they still don't learn the relevant knowledge from all of those weekend courses.

I can't count the times that riders in this latter category have burst into tears in front of me when I've explained that their horse has a stomach condition and the apples they give him every day (with the best of intentions) are unfortunately making it worse.

That the rope halter sold to them in the horsemanship seminar as super horse-friendly was what triggered the recurring blockages in their horse's jaw, poll, neck and shoulder.

That the super horse-friendly open stabling is unfortunately not so super-friendly for their horse after all, because it's being hounded by another horse in the group and is never allowed to rest.

In the course of my work, I've had to deal on a daily basis with the, sometimes significant, adverse consequences, both physical and psychological, that this lack of knowledge has had for the horses.

Most of the blockages, diseases, "behavioural disorders" and organ dysfunctions I've treated in my practice could have been avoided if the riders had known more about the horse and its special characteristics and if horse and rider had been thoroughly trained.

It's possible to cause significant damage to a horse, endangering its mental and physical health, without riding in a single tournament.

Simply because the horse is one of the most sensitive creatures on earth, even if its sheer size and power may belie that sensitivity.

An insecure, nervous rider who compensates for their nerves with tack or a "horseman" who drives his horse endlessly around the round pen for no apparent reason can increase their horse's tension, can inflict blockages, stomach problems, physical damage and mental stress, just as well as a brutal, unprincipled rider who subdues and torments the horse by pulling its nose down to its chest.

Today's horses suffer blockages and injuries when allowed to run loose, simply because they're no longer kept on large pastures in ways appropriate to the species. Because they are ridden solely indoors or on level ground and are always worked in the same way.

Because the variety and versatility needed in training that will keep a horse healthy have become too "dangerous", too time-consuming or too strenuous for the riders.

An old photograph hangs on the wall in my office (Fig. 10). It shows two soldiers with rolled-up shirt sleeves, holding out and crossing their swords. The thin blades meet to form a vertical obstacle around a metre wide and a metre and a half high, barely visible to the human eye. A third soldier and his mount are captured mid-jump.

A large-framed old-school horse, we might say today, attentive and focused, with pointed ears and clearly defined muscles tensed positively in the right places.

The flat leather saddle, with hardly any knee rolls, lies flush against the horse's body on top of a folded woollen blanket held in place by a girth around twenty centimetres wide.

That photo hangs there for one reason and one reason only:

Because it shows that the correct training of rider and horse, the building of confidence, muscle and courage, the forming of a deep partnership between rider and horse, was there in the past.

We already had the right core values in equestrianism; now we just need to bring them out again and pass them on with enthusiasm.

It is high time to banish the new, simpler rules and to bring the old, carefully devised rules and principles back out from those dusty drawers into the light of day.

The training of rider and horse cannot be simplified. Not without the horse suffering.

I hope that, by sharing my experience in this book, I'll be able to raise awareness among riders and owners about how easy it is to harm a horse and how far-reaching the consequences can be.

Fig. 10: Trust, training and partnership: the core values of equestrianism.

Chapter 2

"Once you've had a vet on the yard, you can't get rid of them" – why a once perfectly healthy horse suddenly always has something wrong with it

Some of the connections I came across in my work helped me to resolve one of the main questions that had been bothering me as an active rider since childhood, a question that no-one had ever been able to answer:

Why can't you get rid of a vet once they've been on the yard?

This saying will probably ring a bell with nearly every rider or owner. I remember hearing it in the mouths of horse owners in my childhood. I don't think my grandmother cared for it very much, and interestingly enough it was never the case with her horses, with one exception, but it was certainly true for the other owners and riders in our area.

Year after year, horses would have nothing wrong with them, not a thing. Not even a hoof abscess. And then one day they would come down with a cough or a colic, they would pull a tendon or fracture a splint bone, and after that they would never really recover.

After the first visit, the vet would be a regular sight around the yard, calling several times a month or even a week from then on. And not because the vet was in it for personal gain or did a bad job, but because the horses in question, from the first illness or injury, really did always have "something wrong with them".

What bothered me most about this was the fact that the reasons for the vet's recurring visits usually had nothing to do with the original issue:

A horse that had had colic was suddenly lame in a hind leg a few weeks later. Another got stuck while rolling in his stable and suddenly had trouble with its lateral movements.
A previously very gentle, rideable horse, which had simply slipped and pulled a tendon in its foreleg, suddenly resisted the reins during riding, jerked its head up and started to rear. Even though, after months of rest, the tendon was completely healed and pain-free. Then the horse ended up lame on the other foreleg.
A horse that had recovered from a persistent abscess in the hind hoof suddenly didn't want to canter on one rein and sagged in the hindquarters in its transitions from canter to trot and from trot to walk; a while later it went lame on the sound hind leg.

Another horse, in which a cough had been treated early and cured, suddenly lost elasticity, lacked impulsion over its back and stumbled a lot, sometimes showing irregularities in its rhythm. And from then on, it came down with a new respiratory infection every few weeks.
I could list hundreds of examples like these.

The owners and vets seemed to be at a loss; they'd keep treating the acute symptoms until they healed, but something new would always crop up.
To me, it was one of the greatest mysteries of the equine world. So you can imagine how relieved I was to find connections that explained the vast majority of these chains of events.

Many of the discoveries I made were in "Monday horses": horses that are out of sorts all the time.
Sometimes it's a cough, then a fungal infection, then a hoof abscess, then, despite professional treatment, recurring blockages in certain joints and vertebrae, tendon damage, inflammation in the back, and so on.
Horses like these have often exhausted the conventional forms of treatment, so I have met a lot of them in the course of my career.
In some cases, it was actually a malformation in the cervical spine, an undiagnosed metabolic condition, or some other congenital disorder, that triggered the symptoms.

But in the vast majority of cases, there was an underlying cause that could be remedied.

And so, slowly but surely, more and more links and connections came to light and all of those cases from my childhood and teenage years were explained.

It dawned on me that the horse with colic that went lame in a hind leg a few weeks later might have developed a blockage of the junction between thoracic and lumbar spine when rolling repeatedly during its colic, something many horses do to relieve abdominal pain. This had then caused other lumbar vertebrae to become restricted too, affecting the horse's stifle in turn. Then the lameness in the stifle had been treated, but not the blockages in the spine. And so the cycle began.

The horse with the tendon injury, the one that had suddenly lost its gentle, friendly nature and started to refuse and rear, might have had a blockage in the last two cervical vertebrae and the shoulder. From there, the restriction of movement had possibly progressed to the hyoid bone and then to the temporomandibular joints and up to the sacroiliac joints. The horse's nature hadn't changed at all, it was just suffering from pain in its jaw and its hyoid and its pelvis...
And so on, one case after another.

In the course of my work, I have stood countless times in front of riders or owners who were stunned when I explained to them that their horse's respiratory disease, which had dragged on for months and run out of treatment options, would very likely not go away as long as its withers remained restricted.

That they could have their horse's stomach problems treated with expensive medication time and again, but that this wouldn't produce a lasting improvement until the causes of the horse's enormous stress were eliminated.

That their mare's "moodiness" wasn't "just her character" (this was their explanation, because ovarian cysts found in a thorough investigation had been treated with hormones), but that lasting treatment success could probably be achieved in this case only if the horse's lumbar spine was treated too.

When these people found themselves with a brand new horse after successful treatment, following months and sometimes years of problems, they always asked the same question:

"Why didn't someone tell me this sooner?" The answer is simple. For the same reason that no-one could ever answer my question:

Because almost nobody knows.

For a while in such cases I thought that the vet had simply done a bad job or the wrong treatment had been chosen, the horse hadn't been rested long enough, or something along similar lines.

It was not until after my observations and experience with these horses that it dawned on me that it wasn't the fault of the vet, unsuitable treatment or inadequate care of the horse.

To sum up this topic in advance:

1 It's not a figment of our imagination when horses like these suddenly always have something wrong with them.

2 A blocked sixth and seventh cervical vertebrae, for example, can prevent tendon damage in the forehand from healing and re-exacerbate it each time training is resumed. A blockage in the withers can prevent a full recovery in the case of respiratory conditions or encourage them in the first place. A blocked lumbar vertebra can contribute to reproductive disorders and delay recovery, and there are many more examples.

3 A painful condition will always lead to some sort of sparing or relieving posture. Other structures in turn will then be overloaded to compensate for the body part affected by pain.

   More and more blockages will develop, even if the pain originated in just one. In addition, strain and/or overburdening can lead to other conditions of the musculoskeletal system, such as inflamed tendons or joints, which in turn predisposes to arthritis and cartilage damage in the long term, in short: chronic conditions and various kinds of wear and tear.

4   Blockages in the musculoskeletal system can not only cause lameness, movement disorders and rideability problems, but also trigger dysfunctions or diseases of the organs. The latter, conversely, can lead to significant problems in the musculoskeletal system, not only because of the resulting blockages, but also the associated pain.

5   The psychological aspect of pain as a stress factor for the horse (a prey animal) is often underestimated. The resulting increase in stress levels alone can permanently and effectively suppress the horse's immune system, which naturally makes the horse susceptible to any trigger of disease, no matter how small.

When I wrote at the outset that it is very easy to harm a horse, this is exactly what I meant:

It is possible to inflict a stomach ulcer or inflammatory bowel disease or a skin condition on your horse without riding it in a single competition or exposing it to any major stress or demand.

Now let's take a closer look at why this is the case.

For simplicity, we will work our way through the horse from front to back. This order is purely practical and is not intended as a judgement on the importance of any single connection.

The first connection we'll discuss is the horse's fight or flight instinct and its effects on the body.

Chapter 3

The fight or flight instinct – why it's so important to avoid stress in horses

Some time ago I was giving riding lessons to a friend's five-year-old daughter, on her pony that was actually still much too big for her.

When for the umpteenth time the pony tried to "cut the corners", I told her to go ahead and give it a thump with her inside leg so it would stay out on the track.

She looked at me in horror.

"No!" she said firmly.

Astonished, I asked why not – to me, it was perfectly normal that some ponies sometimes need a thump.

"Because he's my friend," the little girl said, obviously very surprised I was asking her such a stupid question.

Then she rode forward into the middle of the school and explained to me in no uncertain terms:

"If he doesn't want to go into the corners, he's either scared or I can't ride well enough yet for him to understand me."

I tell this story because it illustrates so brilliantly what every rider should in fact do every day: remember why they originally wanted to learn to ride.

Remember how they would stroke other people's horses and dream of having a pony of their own one day. How they would spend hours grooming coats and tying braids and oiling hooves. How they would sneak into their favourite horse's stall for comfort when they were sad. How a soft horsey nose would nuzzle gently into their necks with a reassuring snort. How happy and lucky they were to have a horse for a friend.

Every rider should remember that it was the love of horses that originally made them a rider.

Not a craving for success at the expense of the horse's welfare, not the urge to make money with the horse, not the desire to exercise power over the horse. But a pure, genuine love for these kind, gentle and powerful creatures.

If you see your horse as a friend, you'll do him no harm, you'll look for the faults in yourself and work on your own knowledge and skills to treat the horse in the best possible way.

For me, nothing brings this home better than the little girl's refusal to "hurt" her pony, as she saw it, or her answer to my silly question.

To be as sure as you can that you're not harming your friend the horse, it helps to know as much as possible about his special characteristics.

All the more so because sadly the sheer size and power of horses makes many people forget what extremely sensitive creatures they are (Fig. 11).

An incredible number of links and connections exist between individual joints, muscles, the mind, the nervous system and the organs, all of which play a crucial role in the health and well-being of the horse.

However, these connections exist not only between individual body parts and organ systems; they also encompass sensations such as fear, excitement and stress, and of course the horse's natural instincts.

Not only is the horse "not a robot"; it is also an extremely gentle herbivore and a defensive prey animal, which has good reason to be wary. Just as much now as it was a thousand years ago, a crucial instinct is therefore ingrained into every horse to ensure its survival: the fight or flight instinct.
This instinct affects the horse as a whole and comes into play much more often than most riders realise, so it is vital for us to understand it in order to train and keep a horse healthily.
That makes this the first "connection" we will discuss.

Basically, "fight or flight" is an age-old instinct designed to ensure the horse's survival. Its content is fairly simple: if danger threatens, run away as fast as you can. If you can't escape, fight until you break free. Or until you die.

Fig. 11: Friendship and trust as the basis of every
interaction with the gentle creature that is the horse.

The fight or flight instinct is so strong in the horse that several of its senses are specifically geared to it: the horse hears much better than humans and on completely different frequencies; it can see much further, but almost nothing in its immediate vicinity; it has an acute sense of smell; and it can "read" emotions in other living beings.

A horse can perceive the tiniest signs of tension, fear or excitement in the creatures around it. This includes other horses, dogs, cats, mice, wild animals, birds – or even people.

Simply perceiving such tension gives a horse an instinctive "heads-up" of imminent danger and shifts it automatically into the first stage of the flight or fight instinct.

It can happen as easily as that.

To illustrate the strength of this ability in the horse, I'd like to tell you about an experiment (https://pubmed.ncbi.nlm.nih.gov/19394879/).

Horses and riders were fitted with straps to monitor their heartrates, then the riders were instructed to ride around an arena at one side of which a person was standing with a rolled-up umbrella.

For a few circuits of the track, the heartrates of horses and riders were recorded to establish a baseline: all of the heartrates were calm.

Now the riders were told that the person with the umbrella would open it up with a jerk the next time the horse and rider approached.

In every case, the rider's heartrate soared in anticipation of the shock this would cause to their horse.

And here comes the remarkable part:

The horses' heartrates rose in parallel with those of their riders, without the horses knowing that the umbrella would be opened on the next pass and indeed without it being opened at all.

For the horses, absolutely nothing had changed; they simply responded to the increased tension of the people on their backs.

For me, this experiment illustrates very impressively the extent of truth there is in the old adage that every rider will have heard at some point: "Horses can sense fear in a rider."

This statement is much more than just a typical riding instructor's comment; in fact, it's vitally important.

Because a fearful, insecure rider can put their horse under stress by their own tension alone: the horse perceives the rider's insecurity, anxiety or tension and freezes in anticipation of something bad, ready to flee at any time.

This is why anyone who really is afraid should not get on a horse; such a "test of courage" or false vanity can quickly turn dangerous.

Of course, it's just as easy to put a horse into fight or flight mode and hence under increased stress by using coercion and force. As we've already seen with coercive methods such as Rollkur/LDR, sharp bridles, etc., which are part of normal "training and competition routine" in many stables today, these can inflict considerable and lasting damage on a horse, both physical and mental.

However, it is a widespread misconception that stress is something that only affects show horses and "sport horses", i.e. horses that take part in competition.
There's no doubt that the use of coercion and force, poor husbandry and overwork are effective triggers of stress in the horse.
But a horse in an open stable can suffer just as much from permanently high stress levels as a horse that is continually being forced by its rider to deliver top performance.
A tyrannical neighbour in the next stall or a prickly pasture buddy is just as likely to put a horse under stress as a permanently tense, insecure, anxious rider. Pain produces stress in the horse, just as much as overwork or coercion.
So there's no need to bridle and "ride" a horse the way that many of today's equestrian sport stars unfortunately like to do, or to fly it around the world every weekend, to put it under stress: it's quite enough to have a rider who is uneasy when handling the horse, unknowingly causes it pain or sends out unclear signals. It's enough to have a mean stablemate who terrorises it at every opportunity. A horse that is ridden out and worked on the ground only occasionally can suffer from stress-related stomach ulcers just as much as the horses of some competition riders.

Similarly, a horse can compete successfully without being stressed. Provided it has been prepared for the task with patience and common sense and has a reliable relationship of trust with its rider.

In a nutshell: not every horse that is ridden in competition is stressed and not every horse that lives in an open stable 24/7 is relaxed.

When it comes to the adverse consequences of stress for the horse, most riders think of stomach disorders first. But these are by no means the only consequence.
Stress can also permanently increase the tension in the horse's muscles and suppress the immune system.
A stressed horse won't achieve suppleness or build muscle and will adopt relieving postures in an attempt to avoid pain in the stiff muscles.
This then leads to compensatory blockages, inflammation and wear and tear, which in turn can cause pain and further fuel the horse's stress, as pain is a major trigger of stress.

Suppression of the immune system is also a crucial aspect because it means a significant impairment of the horse's health.

The horse may succumb to literally every fungal infection, every cough, every respiratory infection, every bug doing the rounds, and its health may be seriously affected due to what are actually trivial triggers.

So it is vital to identify and eliminate the causes of stress.

You should of course refrain from any form of coercion or force, allow the horse to run loose at least in the daytime in pastures that are appropriately grassed and fenced for horses (by this I don't mean a paddock the size of a hand towel), make sure he has stablemates or pasture buddies he gets on with, and avoid handling horses if you're actually afraid of them.

Plus it's absolutely essential to work on increasing the horse's stress tolerance, because this automatically lowers its stress levels. Or rather, doesn't ramp them up with every noise, every umbrella and every trip in the trailer.

You can make a brave, "bombproof" police horse out of any horse – all it takes is patience, knowledge and time.

(More on that in *"Reitsport – Auf dem Rücken des Pferdes"* / *"Equestrian sport – On the horse's back"*)

If something triggers the fight or flight instinct, an automatic response kicks in. None of what happens next is actively controlled by the horse; it is all completely automatic. Probably everyone has seen a horse in flight mode at some point.

An example: Imagine we're entering a large meadow on a windy day. The horse grazing there didn't see us coming and couldn't hear us because of the wind.

When it notices us, it jerks its head up and canters away at full tilt across the meadow, with its muscles immediately tensed to the utmost and its tail held erect (Fig. 12) After a hundred metres or so it stops, with its head held high and body tensed to breaking point, points its ears in our direction, draws in a sharp, audible breath and snorts it out again, "hops" on the spot on stiff legs, prances in a semicircle in both directions, starting and stopping, tail down, head carried as high as possible, ears in constant motion, loudly snorting its breath in and out.

The instant the horse recognises us as its friends with the carrots, the tension suddenly falls away, its head sinks forward and down, it gives itself a shake, the tail swings loosely and the muscles relax, especially the back muscles. Our horse canters again to come over and greet us and polish off his carrots, but this canter looks nothing like the last one.

The horse approaches in a relaxed, easy canter, snorting loudly, falls into a quiet trot and then into walk, comes to a halt in front of us, gets his carrot, stays happily beside us, lowers his head and resumes his leisurely grazing.

Fig. 12: Horse in fight or flight mode.

What we have just observed is the first stage of the flight or fight instinct, and also its end. The end is of special importance, because for many horses this state never really comes to an end.

But first things first: when the fight or flight instinct is triggered, large amounts of stress hormones are automatically released into the bloodstream. These lead to an increase in respiratory rate and heartrate, increased blood supply to the muscles, and reduced supply to organs that are not important for flight or fight, such as the skin or digestive system.
The immune system is also shut down so as not to waste energy.
At this point, it's all about survival.
The muscles immediately tense to their utmost, especially those of the hindquarters, in order to get the horse's engine going quickly and efficiently, but the back muscles are under high tension too.
The head is carried as high as possible to expand the field of vision.
The brain shuts down to reptilian level, so the horse doesn't start thinking about whether to run away to the right or the left, but just runs.

This state is perfect for a short and effective flight or a short and effective fight.

But for an hour's schooling under a rider or even as an ongoing, permanent situation, it is a disaster.
This automatic response state in the horse is terminated only by the end of the danger or threat.

Just as it was with our horse in the meadow when he recognised us.

The horse can't simply decide to stop being stressed now; this only happens when the danger or stress trigger is no longer present.

So some horses suffer permanently from an increased stress level.

More on this shortly.

Let's start with a reminder of the processes that happen automatically in a horse in fight or flight mode, the responses that are ingrained in his core and have been since prehistoric times.

If something triggers the horse's flight instinct, such as pain, a noise, or something it sees:

- The muscles tense to the utmost
- The head is raised as high as possible to enable the horse to see better
- The horse tries to escape by running away

If it is prevented from doing so, the second stage of the instinct kicks in: fight until it breaks free or dies.

Now let's imagine how most riders instinctively react when their horse spooks at something: they immediately take up the reins and stop the horse from running.

Which in itself isn't bad as a purely reflexive reaction, as long as they stay calm, relax the reins again immediately and at the same time manage to convince their horse that there's no danger.

But for many riders this is not the case:
They are already uneasy, take fright themselves the moment the horse spooks, and tug on the reins all the harder the more the horse tries to jump aside, turn or run away.

The pressure in the poll caused by this tugging on the reins, and also on the throat due to the curvature of the neck, increases the horse's stress and anxiety in this situation.

Remember, in this moment it is under the control of an age-old instinct associated with threats such as the pressure of a predator's jaws around its poll or throat.

It's fairly certain that a horse in this instinctive flight mode won't stop to think whether the pressure comes from the rider gripping onto the reins and trying to hold it back, or from an attacking predator.

The fact is, and you can easily try this for yourself, the flight/fight mode doesn't come to an end until the horse can lift its head as high as it wants to and look around in peace. Only this can convince it that there is no danger; only this can bring the state of increased tension to an end.

I know this is hard to master for most riders, but in "dangerous" situations it pays off to leave the reins long, I mean really long, no pressure on the bit, and to ride coolly and calmly past the hulking cows or yapping dogs or scary tractors. The more we can make the horse feel that he can decide for himself, almost giving him the security to make the right decision, i.e. not turn round and run for home, the quicker the fight or flight instinct will be over.

Just as a bolting horse is brought back under control by – ironically – vigorously driving it on, a soothing word, tapping techniques, loose but reassuring legs and definitely a loose rein can often help here.

I would advise against doing this experiment if the horse is actually panicky.

What I mean is this: a horse is "afraid" of dogs and as soon as the rider spots a dog somewhere in the distance, he automatically shortens the reins as much as he can because he's waiting for the horse to jump aside or turn round. By doing this, he increases the horse's uneasiness, making the situation worse.

He should take a reliable lead horse with him the first few times, definitely keep the reins loose and stay relaxed. It's a dog, not a sabre-toothed tiger.

Now let's imagine that a horse bridled with draw-reins or ridden in LDR, with a clearly under-skilled or even fearful rider on its back, suddenly spooks at something.
The automatic instinct kicks in and the horse wants to lift its head quickly to locate the danger, but is denied the motion by the draw-reins pulling his nose down to his chest.
In its struggle to raise its head to expand its field of

vision, the horse feels enormous pressure on its sensitive poll.

As it can't get free, it can't assess the danger as having passed, so its muscles remain under high tension and it keeps instinctively fighting the pressure on its poll and jaw, so as to at least visually locate and classify the danger.

Just in this one situation, we can inflict blockages on our horse that can lead to organ diseases and severe lameness.

Even if we dismount after an hour's riding and the horse eventually calms down in its stall, the damage is already done.

Now let's imagine that this state doesn't end but continues; to keep things simple, we'll pick out just four aspects:

1. The stress hormones suppress the immune system.
2. The muscles become highly tensed.
3. The blood supply to the digestive system is restricted.
4. The brain shuts down to reptilian level.

The minimum consequences of this are that:

1   The horse becomes susceptible to every cough, disease or fungal infection going.
2   It can't build up new muscle, and existing muscles become painfully over-acidified.
3   It develops stomach ulcers, faecal water and colic.

4   Learning and complex performances are impossible.

I'd like to try to illustrate this with what is unfortunately a true-life story:

A rider buys a new horse and decides to keep it at a stables where her old horse and several other horses are already standing. (Standing is the right word, because grazing is only provided by the hour.)
From his very first day, our horse is constantly being threatened by his neighbours on either side.
When the feed cart arrives, they kick at the box walls and bite the bars, flattening their ears.
So our horse has arrived in an unfamiliar new environment, he's already stressed and now he's under constant attack from the horses beside him.
It's not a huge leap to assume that this situation puts our horse in permanent fear of injury and thus under constant stress. The danger is never over = the horse is in an ongoing flight mode.
Once a day the rider shows up, fetches the horse from his box and slams the saddle down on his aching back. Remember, he hasn't had a minute to relax, his muscles are permanently tensed in anticipation of flight or fight, and tense muscles, as we all know, are very painful.
The pain caused by the poorly fitting saddle (a hand-me-down from the old horse) and the rider's weight is another trigger for the flight instinct.
All of the reactions described above are now back in full force in our horse.

However, he can't lift his head because the rider pulls it down into his chest.

This further restricts his field of vision; he can see next to nothing and his stress level rises because he can't look around freely, as this automatic response demands, and so he can't assess the risk.

Now maybe an obstacle falls over, our horse spooks, wanting to escape the new danger, again he can't lift his head but feels increasing pressure in his poll, one of two sites that a predator would seize in order to kill him.

The second site, the throat, is constricted by the forced, chest-biting posture in which the rider is "training" him...

So our horse has to perform at his best for an hour under the utmost tension.

Lap after lap, the rider calls for difficult exercises and asks our horse to learn new things as well.

Unfortunately, she fails to notice that her horse doesn't achieve even a hint of suppleness at any point during their riding.

She doesn't know any different, that's how everyone rides at these stables.

When the hall door slams, our horse leaps forward, the stress has become too much, he just wants to escape the danger, any way he can. But for our horse, this "escape attempt" ends with the rider digging her spurs into his sensitive flanks while pulling so hard on his mouth that the bit tears open the soft downy corners of his mouth and crushes his tongue.

After an hour, the rider puts our horse back in his

box, where he is immediately pestered again by the neighbours. Every muscle aches and so do his poll, mouth and back, he's exhausted and would love to rest, but he can't calm down. The processes in his body are still running in "flight mode". Remember, this state doesn't end until the danger has passed.

Among other things, this means that our horse's immune system and digestive tract are not working as they should.

Our horse develops stomach ulcers, which in turn cause pain, further increasing his stress level.

The rider still doesn't notice any of this, she just wonders why her horse is losing weight and passing faecal water.

"Must be the haylage," say the other stable users. "He'll have to get used to it."

She buys new saddle pads and matching bandages and ear veils to ease her conscience (see how much she spends on her horse) and maybe also to distract from his slightly unattractive condition, and continues to "ride" blithely for an hour every day.

Still with the same badly fitting, painful saddle, the same constant pressure, the same over-flexed neck that causes stress and pain and doesn't allow the horse's back to loosen at any time.

Nothing changes in the horse's living conditions either.

Now our horse develops a persistent fungal infection. The rider gets annoyed and contacts the previous owner, accusing him of selling her an infected horse, which the owner denies.

And rightly so, because not a single horse in his

stable is infected and our horse has been with his new owner for months now.

The rider gets shampoo and creams from the vet and washes and treats the infection, but new patches keep appearing.

When autumn brings the first respiratory infection into the stables, our horse is among the first to start coughing.

The rider still fails to see any connection with the horse's immune system having been weakened by the constant stress. She sends for the vet again, treats the symptoms again, and gets annoyed about this "frail and sickly horse".

One winter night, our horse gets a colic and dies. The rider stands beside him and cries, saying she just can't understand it, she did everything she could for her horse, just recently she spent another few hundred on vet bills and new tack and so on.

I had asked this rider some questions at the time. The conversation went like this and is a good example of its kind (of which I've had many).

Question: "Why don't you turn your horse out to pasture?"

Answer: "What a funny question – no-one does that! Not even the professionals! They only hurt themselves on pasture!"

Question: "Why don't you insist that your horse stand next to horses that are friendly to him?"

Answer: "What sort of airy-fairy nonsense is that!

The horse has his box, end of story!"
Question: "Why don't you learn to ride rather than forcing your horse's nose onto his chest?"
Answer: "That's typical jealousy again, showing through questions like that! Just because I ride better than you, you query my training methods!"
Question: "Why don't you get a saddler in?"
Answer: "The saddle's brand new, there's nothing wrong with it! I had it made just recently for my last horse."
Question: "But then it fitted your last horse, not this one... Where *is* your last horse?"
Answer: "He had to be put to sleep."
Question: "Oh, I'm sorry to hear that. Was he very old?"
Answer (snappish): "No, he was eight. But he had colic."

And even that – the fact that this was now the second horse to die in the same way under her care – hadn't given this rider any cause to think. She was simply completely convinced she was doing the right thing.
Because that's what everyone does at these stables. And their style of riding can be seen everywhere (and working successfully) at international shows. Shifting baselines.

She thought her behaviour was normal, simply didn't know any better, and had no interest in expanding her knowledge.

It is precisely this lack of knowledge, sadly a theme running through many areas of equestrian sport today, that is the main reason for the horses' suffering.

Which is why such examples are also seen in open stables, where horses can't cope with the constant "vulnerability" (yes, some horses apparently prefer to sleep in a safe, spacious, dry loose-box bedded with soft fragrant straw) and/or are put under permanent stress, usually by a quarrelsome troublemaker. By the way, it is not uncommon for this poorly socialised animal to belong to the stable owner and for the owners of its thin, bitten victims, cautiously inquiring if there's any chance of isolating the troublemaker, to be told:
"Absolutely not. Your horse will just have to stand up for itself."

There are examples of horses whose owners make them do lap after lap of the round pen, assuming this is horse-friendly because they've seen it on YouTube under "Horsemanship", or who canter around the training arena for thirty minutes once a week solely in Western canter or lope (because that's the most comfortable), without their horse or even themselves being trained in any way.

There are examples of horses whose riders or owners are actually afraid, but for some unfathomable reason desperately want a horse. With the result that the horse becomes ever more insecure, stressed and aggressive due to its owner's fear.

Kindness and carrots are sadly not enough; the human being needs to be a leader for their horse, someone who can be relied upon in tricky situations. Of course, not all of these examples end in a fatal colic, but many horses suffer from years of stress and the associated adverse consequences for their health and well-being. And that alone cannot be in the interests of a real rider. In my view it's important to understand this:

A horse doesn't have to be panicky to suffer from increased stress levels, and this state may not be apparent in many horses at first glance.

But continually high stress prevents the horse from relaxing, impairs its well-being and sooner or later leads to disease. Both of the organs and of the musculoskeletal system.

Many of the mistakes made today at the expense of horse health could be avoided by following clear and simple rules.

At this point I'd like to share one of these rules with you: you should never start a fight with your horse. If you're not getting anywhere with a horse, you should immediately lay the reins on its neck and take a break. Walk out of the arena on a long rein, praise the horse, put him back in his box or turn him back out to grass, then start over again the next day – and work smarter this time.

Because of course it's not the horse's fault if the

rider asks for something he doesn't understand or isn't capable of performing.
It's the rider's responsibility to make sure at all times that they train and work with the horse in such a way that he can do what is asked of him.

The little girl had already understood this correctly (Fig. 13).

Fig. 13: Look for the fault in yourself and take responsibility: two key basic rules for every rider that you can't learn early enough. Actually, two rules that everyone should take to heart, whether they're a rider or not...

Chapter 4

The hyoid bone and its connections – what the hyoid bone has to do with dehydration and forehand lameness

The horse's hyoid bone is a bony structure comprised of several articulated joints. It hangs like a swing from the horse's temporal bones between the branches of the lower jaw.
The front part of this structure (or "apparatus") forms an extension that stabilises and moves with the tongue, while the rear part connects to the larynx among other things (Fig. 14).

If the hyoid bone cannot move both up and down and forwards and backwards at the point where it connects to the skull, and move freely to and fro with the tongue, or if the mobility in both joints is disrupted, this also restricts the mobility of the larynx and uvula, impeding the act of swallowing.
In extreme cases, horses may be reluctant to drink and have trouble eating, and drooling is often seen in horses with a restricted or blocked hyoid.
To explain it very simply: as everyone knows, you can only ever swallow *or* breathe. If we try to do both at the same time, we choke.

The reason for this is a valve system formed by the epiglottis, a flap in the throat that prevents food from entering the trachea (windpipe). The trachea always stands open, and food can enter the oesophagus only when the tongue is pushed up during swallowing.

For this mechanism to work fully and freely, the horse's hyoid apparatus needs to be able to move within its physiological limits.

If this is not the case, swallowing is still possible but comes with increased muscle tension, which in turn is likely to be at least uncomfortable, if not painful. Precisely what a tight, overcompensating muscle feels like.

Swallowing becomes so unpleasant that it is avoided if at all possible. For the horse, this often results in dehydration and physical deterioration.

And also stomach problems, because saliva, the only natural buffer the horse has to counteract its stomach acid, is only produced when the horse chews and of course only enters the stomach if it can be swallowed.

More about that later, but for now just this:

If your horse has had a blocked hyoid bone for some time, watch out for symptoms that might point to a stomach condition. These are listed in Chapter 11.

Some horses with a fixed hyoid apparatus will also leave their concentrate feed, which I believe is due to a fear of choking.

The fact is: a blockage of this tiny bony structure causes some horses to stop drinking almost entirely and become dehydrated.

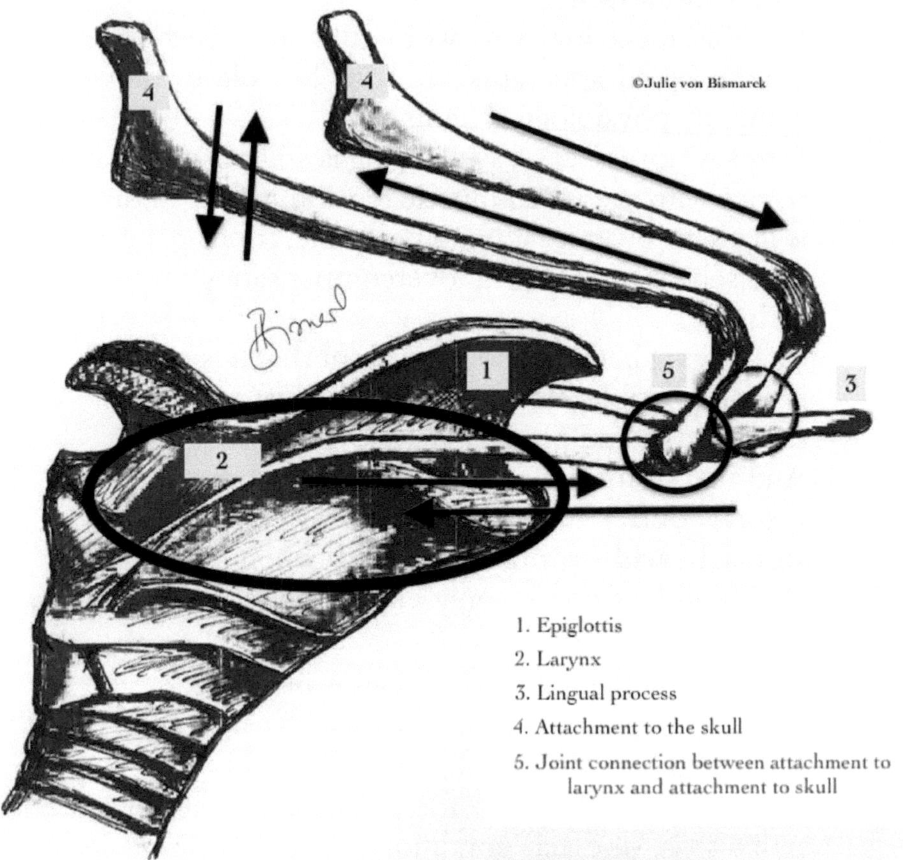

Fig. 14: The hyoid bone and its connections.

The first time I identified this connection between a restricted hyoid bone and swallowing was while treating a horse that I'd been called out to because of general "tension".

While examining the horse I noticed (in fact only by chance) early signs of dehydration.
The owner told me that the horse hadn't been worked hard lately because its "tension" made it so unrideable; it had just been investigated by a vet and had no known conditions.
Various blockages were present, but an apparently long-standing blockage of the hyoid bone stood out in particular.
The entire hyoid apparatus was completely fixed and immobile.

Even as I set about mobilising it, the horse began to salivate freely, and then to swallow and chew.

Once I'd released all the structures involved in the hyoid blockages and started treating the horse's other blockages, he opened his mouth as wide as it would go and moved his tongue from side to side for about a minute using huge, over-exaggerated movements, rolling it back and forth and sticking it out as far as he could.

He licked and rolled and twisted his tongue as if it had suddenly regained feeling or as if he could move it properly again for the first time in ages. It was absolutely fascinating.
I don't know if you've ever had anything to do with giraffes, but it strongly reminded me of giraffes in

Africa, my second home, stripping the fresh leaves off acacia trees with their fifty-centimetre tongues after the rains had come to the veldt.

It was the most extraordinary reaction to a hyoid treatment that I'd ever seen.

The restriction must have been causing the horse enormous suffering.

When we turned the horse back out to grass after treatment, it made a bee-line for the water tub and drank it almost dry.

That was when I realised there might be a connection between the blocked hyoid and the horse's dehydration. And therefore between the act of swallowing and the fixed hyoid bone.

From then on, I paid special attention to any horse that showed a blockage of the hyoid bone, looking for signs of difficulty in swallowing or inadequate fluid intake, and I asked the owners about their horses' drinking behaviour.

It soon emerged that this connection existed in almost every horse.

But a blocked hyoid bone can not only stop the horse from eating and drinking properly, it can also cause forehand lameness – through its connection to the shoulder.

One of the muscles that pulls the tongue back to allow swallowing is the omohyoid or "shoulder hyoid muscle" (Fig. 15).

This muscle originates under the shoulder blade in the shoulder fascia and attaches to the hyoid process of the hyoid bone.

This means that there is a direct connection between the hyoid apparatus and the horse's shoulder.
If this muscle is over-tensed, as in horses ridden in Rollkur/LDR or with tight nosebands or other types of constraint, the tongue stays permanently pulled back.

This naturally restricts first the mobility of the tongue itself, affecting swallowing and eating, and second (as a direct cause-and-effect) the mobility of the shoulder.
Acting through this muscle connection, a fixed hyoid bone can lead to major errors in rhythm, loss of reach, lameness and forehand movement disorders.

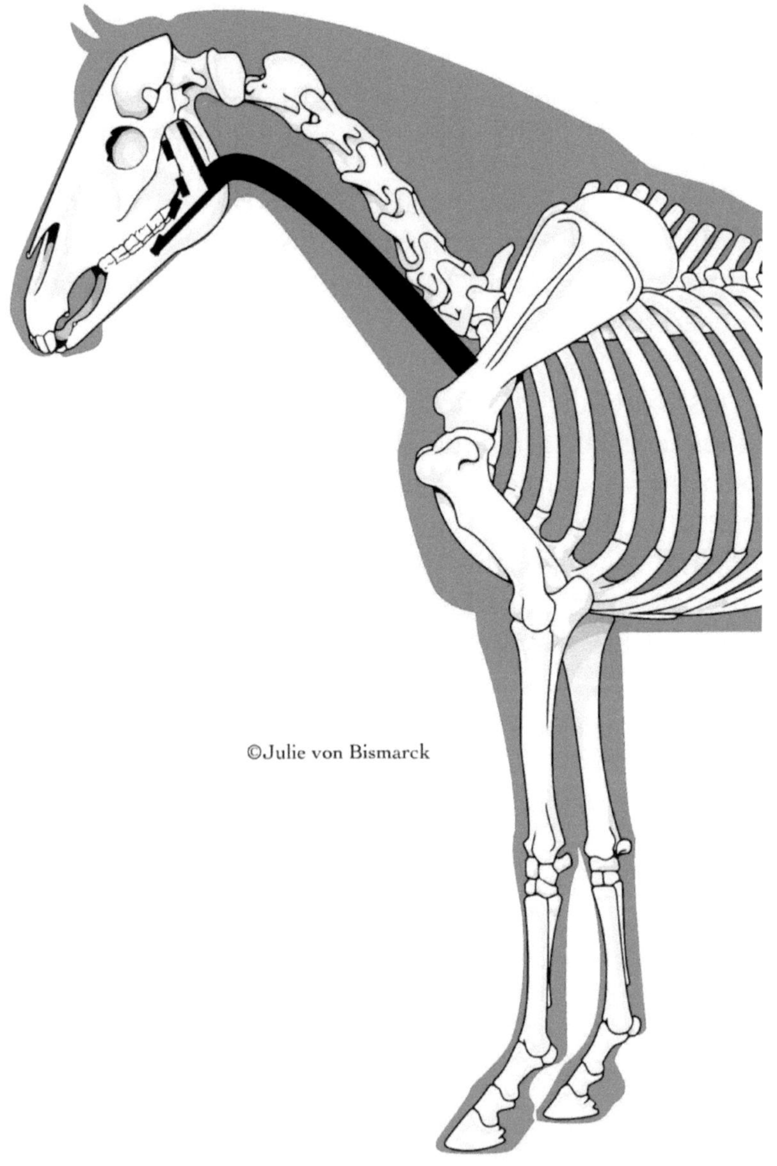

Fig. 15: The omohyoid or "shoulder hyoid" muscle.

As we've already seen, the horse has no bony or joint connection attaching its front legs to its body. The shoulder and humerus are attached to the body by muscles, ligaments and tissues alone, which in principle allows better shock absorption and more flexibility in movement. This makes the shoulder muscles the decisive factor in allowing smooth, flowing movement:

A tight or "stuck" shoulder fascia therefore quickly puts an end to this smooth motion and the shoulder is no longer fully mobile.
This also affects the elasticity of the muscles supporting the trunk between the front legs and the muscles seize, cancelling out the flexible shock-absorbing function. As a result, the horse's movements become "heavy" and into the ground: a finding often referred to as a "blockage of the sternum".

When the horse brings its leg forward (Fig. 16), its shoulder blade slides backwards/down on the thorax and the angle in the shoulder joint, i.e. between shoulder blade and humerus, opens.
When the horse brings its leg back, i.e. in the support phase, the shoulder blade slides forwards/up and the angle in the shoulder joint closes.

If this mobility, this sliding of the shoulder blade on the thorax, is restricted by tension in the shoulder fascia, this has the following consequences:

1 The horse can no longer bring the affected leg forward as far as the "healthy" leg, so it loses reach.

2 In the supporting leg phase, when the weight is on the affected leg, the inhibited forward slide of the shoulder blade causes a painful tension in the muscle groups connecting the front leg to the horse's trunk. This tension extends into the neck and upper back.

You can think of it as an extreme tension in the shoulder and neck area – anyone who spends a lot of time at a computer will know how painful this is. Lameness is an expression of this painful state. The horse goes lame because it tries to minimise the supporting leg phase on the affected leg.

Conversely, a blockage of the shoulder joint can cause a blockage of the hyoid apparatus, even without the rider using any sharp bits, draw-reins or Rollkur, or riding with a hard hand.
I first encountered this connection thanks to one particular patient and found it again later in many other horses:

Once I had a good idea for myself of the importance of hyoid bone blockages in the horse, I did of course watch out very carefully for possible causes of these restrictions.

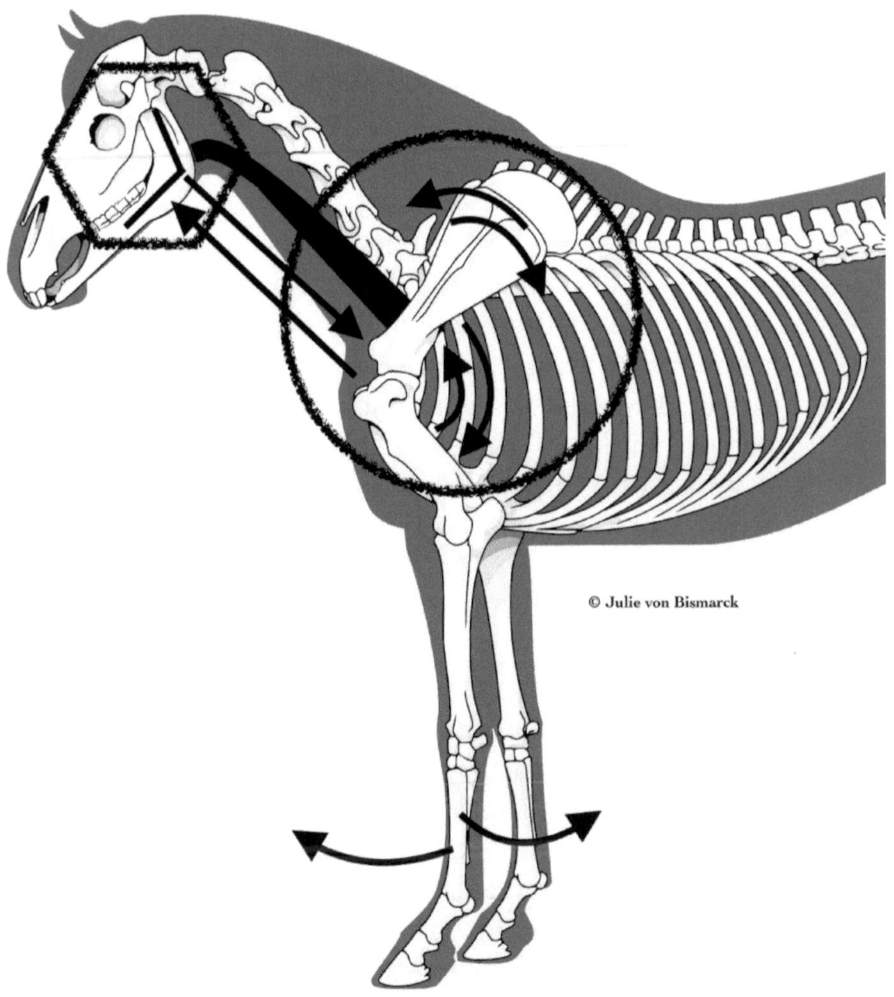

Fig. 16: The shoulder hyoid muscle and the directions of movement of the shoulder and front legs.
When the leg is brought forward, the shoulder blade slides backwards/down and the shoulder joint is extended.
When the leg is brought back, the shoulder blade slides forwards/up and the shoulder joint is flexed.
A tight shoulder hyoid muscle can interfere with this movement.

For quite a while I assumed that most of these blockages were simply caused by bad riding – it was just the most obvious cause, due to the direct action of the bit on the tongue.

But one day I had a patient with a completely immobile hyoid apparatus and as usual I asked about the use of the horse and the style of riding, who trained the horse, and so on.
I expected to hear that the horse was often ridden on a curb bit and "collected" (or what many riders today mean by this...) and was surprised to be told that the horse was only ridden bitless and with a normal noseband.
Without any straps acting on the lower jaw or any lever-action wheels to which the reins were buckled.

So there had to be another cause, and that's when I thought of this particular muscle that originates in the shoulder fascia and attaches to the hyoid bone. As this horse also had a significant shoulder blockage, I suspected a connection.
The owner confirmed that the horse had stepped into a hole on a ride a few weeks earlier and had barely managed to avoid falling, which explained the shoulder block and also suggested an involvement of the shoulder fascia and surrounding tissue.

This inverse connection was confirmed in this first horse, and then over and over again in my examination and treatment of many other horses in the months and years that followed.

So it doesn't have to be a hard hand or bad riding that triggers blockages of the hyoid bone: there might also be conditions of the forehand causing a relieving posture with compensation in the shoulder muscles.

Tendon damage, pododermatitis (inflammation of the hoof corium) or any other painful condition in a foreleg automatically causes the horse to adopt a relieving posture in an attempt to minimise pain.

As a result, the shoulder fascia will tighten, i.e. the origin of the shoulder hyoid muscle, and eventually the muscle itself.

This muscle tension pulls the tongue permanently backwards and we are back to a fixed hyoid apparatus, with the inevitable adverse effects and sometimes dangerous consequences for the horse (swallowing, breathing, drinking, eating...).

So a horse that "pulls up its tongue" or sticks its tongue out might be doing so due to a blockage in the shoulder or an undiagnosed underlying condition of one or both front legs.

When mobilising the hyoid bone, it's always important to treat the origin of the shoulder hyoid muscle in the shoulder fascia as well, otherwise any success will be short-lived.

Blockages of the hyoid bone are unfortunately on the increase, so I'd just like to say one more thing about their causes:

As with blockages of the jaw joints and poll, riding with a hard hand, sharp bits, tight halters or nosebands, forced postures such as Rollkur/LDR or the use of draw-reins are causes that quickly lead to immobility of the hyoid bone.

This applies to every horse and every rider in every discipline: whether it's a Western rider, leisure rider, dressage rider or show jumper who sits on the horse and uses a heavy hand, sharp bit or over-tight bridle, it makes no difference in the end to the health of the horse.

These are some of the symptoms that may point to a blocked hyoid bone:

- Changes in drinking and possibly in feeding behaviour
- A suspected increase in salivation (horse doesn't swallow, so saliva drools from the mouth)
- Tongue pulled up/stuck out
- Head tilting, going behind the reins, lifting head up and going against the reins under the rider and on the lunge
- Short, tight gait
- Forehand movement disorders
- Forehand lameness

If a horse shows one or more of these symptoms, you should get an experienced osteopath to examine its hyoid bone and treat it if necessary.
As mentioned earlier, correct treatment of the hyoid bone should always include treatment of the origin of the shoulder hyoid muscle, or the blockage will quickly return.

An exercise you can use to prevent blockages of the hyoid apparatus is given on the next page.

Exercise to mobilise the hyoid bone and jaw joints:

Place one or more fingers on the bars of the horse's mouth so that it begins to chew.
Allow the horse to move its head freely (don't tether it!) and make sure the halter is loose enough not to restrict the movements of the jaw.
Rope halters are not suitable.
You'll notice that the horse makes ever larger chewing movements and rolls its tongue back and forth.
Keep it moving like this for around a minute.

Always start on one side first, then switch to the other side after a minute or so and repeat the exercise.

This exercise is only suitable as prevention and is not used to treat an actual blockage. If a horse shows strong resistance to this exercise (this doesn't mean defensive reactions due to de-worming or other bad experiences) or significant difficulty in accepting the bit and/or unusual feeding behaviour, get a professional in to treat its hyoid and have the jaw joints checked for more serious conditions.

Checking for dehydration:

Gently pinch and lift a fold of skin at the base of the
horse's neck. When you let go, the fold should bounce
back immediately. If you can still see the fold after
two seconds, this may be a sign of mild dehydration.
If you can still see it after five seconds, you should call
your vet – especially if the horse is also producing
dark urine and hard, round "apples" of manure.

Chapter 5

The temporomandibular joint and sacroiliac joint – how restricted movement in the jaw can put the hindquarters out of action

The temporomandibular joint (TMJ) connects the lower jaw and the temporal bone of the skull. It combines a hinging and a sliding action to allow different movements:

- Forwards and backwards
- Right and left
- Rotating/grinding
-

(See Fig. 17; the joint is not visible because it lies under the bone.)

This mobility is crucial for the horse, not only for chewing, but also for movement.

A blockage of one TMJ tends to extend quickly to the other one too, as the lower jaw (mandible) is fused in the centre below the lower incisors, so its two branches cannot be moved separately.
If they do move separately, the horse should immediately be taken to a veterinary clinic, as this is very likely to mean a broken jaw.

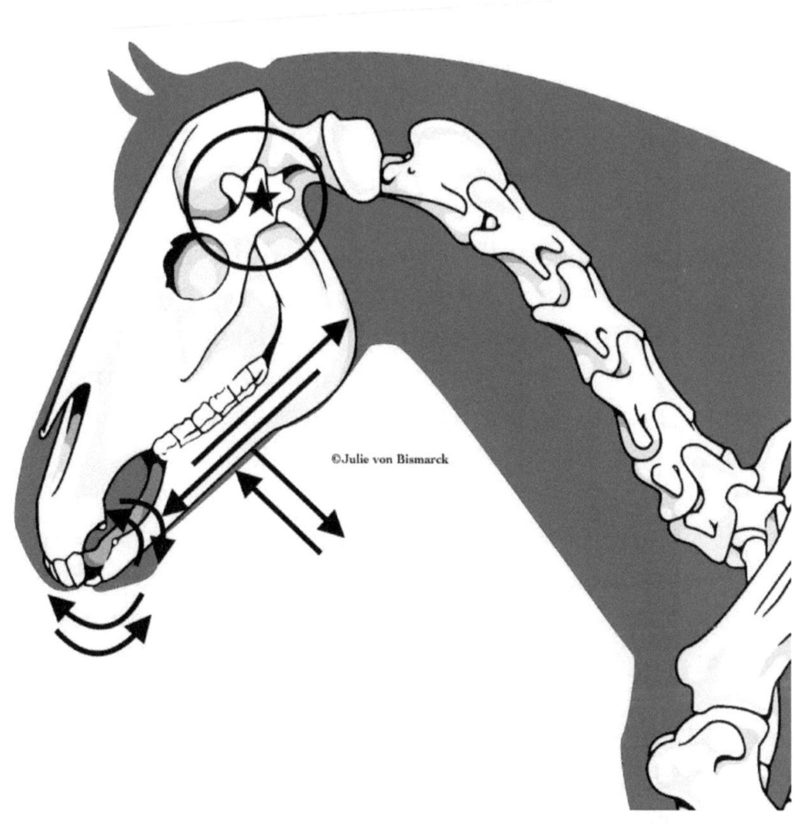

Fig. 17: The temporomandibular joint and its directions of movement.

Horses in the wild rarely get a blocked jaw but if they do it's to compensate for a blockage of the sacroiliac joints (more on this shortly) or due to a dental condition, whereas TMJ blockages are a common finding in riding and carriage horses.
The long lever of the mandibular branches and the position of the bit are assumed to play a decisive role in such blockages:

A downward pull or pressure on the front third of the lower jaw, i.e. the site where not only bits, but also chiffneys (anti-rearing bits), lead ropes, etc. are attached, causes the long mandibular branch to act like a lever, multiplying the forces acting on it many times over (Fig. 18).

This means that the TMJ is put under a pressure it is not designed for. This pressure is absorbed by the muscles, which tense up accordingly and then remain tensed, restricting the mobility of the joint: the TMJ becomes blocked.
A hard hand, forced over-flexion, or a rope pulled through the mouth - e.g.because the horse won't enter the trailer, can cause a permanent blockage of the TMJ within seconds.
Not to mention the other health consequences.

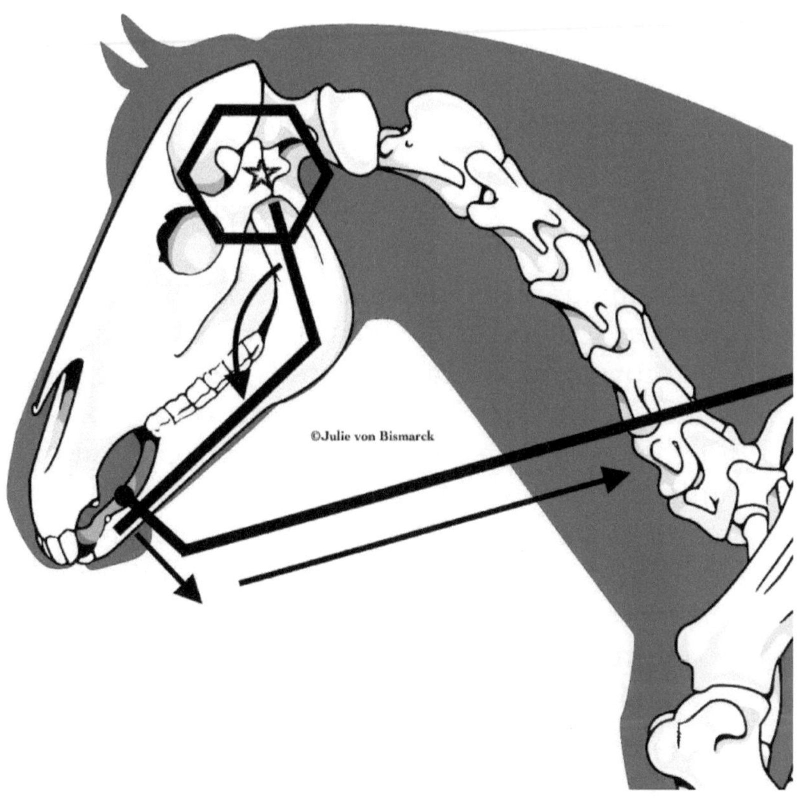

Fig. 18: Lever action on the long mandibular branch puts pressure on the angle of the jaw. As the jaw cannot open here (the bone is continuous), this pressure extends to the TMJ itself. The joint is not designed to take this type of stress, so the surrounding muscles come to the rescue by tensing up, locking the joint (= TMJ blockage).

From this point on, the TMJs no longer have their full range of motion and in severe cases they have none at all.
If we look closely at the natural movements in the TMJ, the far-reaching consequences for the horse of such restricted movement become clear.

1. Pushing the lower jaw forward:

This is an automatic movement in which the lower jaw slides forward as the horse lowers its head.
This movement is geared towards optimising feed intake: the incisors are arranged one on top of the other in order to tear up grass and plants, and at the same time the sliding forward of the lower jaw creates space in the TMJ itself for the grinding movements that are then needed to crush the food.

(If you turn a horse out to grass wearing a halter, always make sure the noseband and throat-lash are loose enough not to hinder the movements of the jaw.)

2. Grinding and lateral movements:

Like many herbivores, the horse chews with a grinding or circular motion, rotating the lower jaw. This crushes the feed between the broad molars, almost like grinding between two millstones.
At the same time, this unique chewing motion mechanically expels saliva from the salivary glands. This is especially important for the horse, as saliva

acts as a natural buffer to neutralise its stomach acid. And since a horse's stomach contains acid all the time, not just when it eats, this buffer is extremely important to stop the acid attacking the stomach lining.

We always need to bear in mind that the horse's body and locomotor system were designed for a life on the plains.
For covering fifteen miles or more per day and spending almost the entire day feeding – on coarse, fibre-rich grass. This again helps us to understand why roughage, i.e. good-quality hay, teff and straw, is so vitally important for the horse: it needs all the chewing movements required to break down this fibre-rich food, simply in order to bring saliva into its stomach and thus protect the stomach from acid.

The lateral movements of the lower jaw to right and left are not just part of chewing; they are also crucial for every turn the horse makes.
This is because it is the lower jaw that initiates any change in the horse's direction of travel, by shifting slightly in the intended direction.

3. Pushing the lower jaw back:

This movement occurs as the horse raises its head. It virtually "closes" the TMJ, making chewing difficult in this position.
The pushing back of the lower jaw brings tension into the horse's neck and back, which extends into

the hindquarters.

In short: when the horse pushes its lower jaw backwards, this movement automatically produces a tense, upright position.

Remember the chapter on the fight or flight instinct: lifting the head not only widens the field of vision, but also brings tension to the hindquarters (the horse's "engine"), to allow an effective, immediate escape from the situation.

In riding, we turn this to our advantage when we ride a horse in an upright, elevated position.

This shows again how cleverly each of the horse's movements are coordinated, no matter how small, and how important they really are.

As these movements are very similar in humans, this gives us an excellent opportunity to see for ourselves what a restriction of these relatively small but crucial movements can mean for a horse.

Try it out; the results are remarkable.

Exercise 1:

Stand up straight but relaxed and soften your jaw slightly: when the jaw is in neutral position, the upper and lower teeth don't meet – the same is true for the horse. Now move your head, chin first, slowly forward-downward without changing anything else. Notice how your lower jaw slides forward with the movement. Close your eyes to feel this sensation better.

Stand up straight again and this time tightly clench your teeth. Now repeat the same movement.
Notice how much tension builds up, extending right down through your neck, and how the movement may even become painful.
The movement is still possible, but it is no longer loose, natural, effortless and flowing.

The same is true for a horse if its lower jaw is prevented from sliding forward.

At this point, another word about the importance of the two-finger rule for buckling the noseband: no-one can expect a loose, smooth, natural movement from a horse whose noseband has been cinched tight.
It is perfectly understandable that the horse would just submit and keep its head low in a "frozen pose", because the dynamics of lowering the head into contact would mean an easy pushing forward of the lower jaw and this is prevented by tying its mouth closed.
Nor can you expect a soft, relaxed contact from a horse that has – say – hooks or waves on its teeth, or arthritis in its TMJ.

<u>Exercise 2:</u>

Stand up straight but relaxed again, soften your jaw and walk forwards normally, turning to the left after a few steps.

Notice how your head initiates the movement and your shoulder and upper spine follow.

But now focus consciously on your lower jaw and notice how it shifts in the intended direction first, even if only slightly, before your head, shoulders and spine then follow.

Now try the same thing again, this time turning to the right; interestingly, the movement is usually "easier" on one side.

Assuming this is also the case for the horse, this is probably another reason why most horses find it so much easier to flex and bend on one rein than on the other.

Now clench your teeth again and repeat the experiment. Notice again how pressure develops throughout your head and how unnatural or mechanical the movement suddenly feels.

Remember this the next time you buckle your noseband or flash strap, as it will definitely encourage you to follow the two-finger rule. Always leave two adult finger-widths between the nose bone and the noseband or strap.

Exercise 3:

Stand up straight but relaxed, soften your jaw and now consciously pull your lower jaw backwards towards the back of your head.

Notice how this movement automatically pulls your head back and puts your neck and upper back under tension = you stand up straight and your body tenses.

This happens in the horse when it lifts its head to look around, like our horse in the meadow.
This mechanism can take the horse from calm, relaxed grazing into a state of high tension, ready to bolt, within a split second. It is also the position in which we ride "in elevation".

Now try exaggerating the movement: pull your lower jaw as far towards the back of your head as possible; the chin automatically goes to the chest and the neck tenses, extending into the upper spine.

This is the position a horse is put in when in Rollkur, LDR or any tight posture (Fig. 19).

Notice how your throat closes up, breathing becomes harder and it takes an effort to swallow.
Now try to chew in this position. Notice how limited the movements are and how much tension you need in your lower neck muscles to perform them at all.

So it won't come as a surprise to learn that swallowing and chewing in this position also blocks the hyoid bone.
I'd be amazed if you can hold this extreme position for more than half a minute.
My neck muscles start to hurt within seconds.

It should be clear by now that pulling a horse's nose down to its chest not only increases its stress levels (it can't see, lift its head or look around and is short of breath because its throat is squeezed), but also prevents saliva from reaching the stomach, because chewing is obstructed and swallowing becomes almost impossible.

We talked about the importance of this buffer earlier, in relation to the hyoid bone, and I describe it in more detail later, so here I'll just say this: stomach ulcers are really not surprising in horses "ridden" in this way, for many reasons.

If we now realise that the horse needs all of these movements in its TMJ just in order to be able to move freely and naturally, we can easily imagine the serious consequences of restricting this mobility.

Whether due to hooks or waves on the teeth, blockages or painful/degenerative conditions of the TMJs, a hard hand, sharp bits, tightly buckled nosebands, Rollkur/LDR, draw-reins, etc., restricted mobility means:

The horse's lower jaw cannot move forward, which means that the horse is unable to supple, even if it is ridden "forward-downward", because this natural movement is prevented by the tight halter, the blockage, the degenerative condition.

It can't chew.

Enormous pressure builds up throughout the head, another reason for the absence of any suppleness.

Fig. 19: Horse in position from Exercise 3.

The horse can't initiate turns naturally because it can't move its lower jaw sideways, which means it goes into the turn with a stiff neck and head/poll, and no flowing, natural movement is possible.
The TMJ is permanently "closed" and tense, which means that the rest of the horse's body can't supple or "let go" either.

In the same way as it's important to buckle the noseband loosely according to the two-finger rule, and to ride the horse in a real forward-downward extension posture, it's also important to have the horse's teeth checked regularly by a specialist equine dentist.
Even the smallest changes in the teeth can block the TMJs, triggering serious problems.

This is because the consequences of restricted movement in the TMJs extend beyond those already discussed above:

The TMJs are connected to the sacroiliac joints and their influence therefore extends right into the pelvis.
A blockage of a TMJ leads sooner or later to a blockage of the sacroiliac joint on the other side of the body, and vice versa (Fig. 20).
This means that restricted movement in the TMJ can not only trigger the problems described above, but also paralyse the entire pelvis and the transmission of thrust and impulsion from the hindquarters to the back.

This is another reason why horses ridden with a hard hand and a tightly closed mouth, or even in forced over-flexion, can never be supple.

Let's take a look at the biomechanics:

The sacroiliac joints (Fig. 21) are the only connection between the pelvis, i.e. the hindquarters, and the horse's back. They are not true joints, but a connection consisting of taut ligaments, tissues and muscles between the underside of the iliac crest and the sacrum.

Due to the enormous forces that act and are transmitted here, the range of motion in the sacroiliac joints is very small, benefiting stability.

Mobility in the sacroiliac joints, i.e. a tiny but measurable spring-like motion of the iliac blades in the connections to the sacrum (one right, one left) formed by ligaments and muscles, is therefore of crucial importance, as it is here that thrust is transmitted from the hindquarters to the spine.

It can be imagined like this:

The weight-bearing hind leg pushes off and the resulting impulsion/thrust reaches the pelvic ring via the hip joint.

The ilium compresses forwards and down with the movement at the sacrum, the last part of the horse's spine before the tail vertebrae = when the hind leg pushes off, backwards and out, transferring the thrust/impulsion from the ilium/pelvic ring to the sacrum and from there to the lumbar spine. In the lead phase and when the foot takes off, the ilium springs backwards/upwards in the sacroiliac joint.

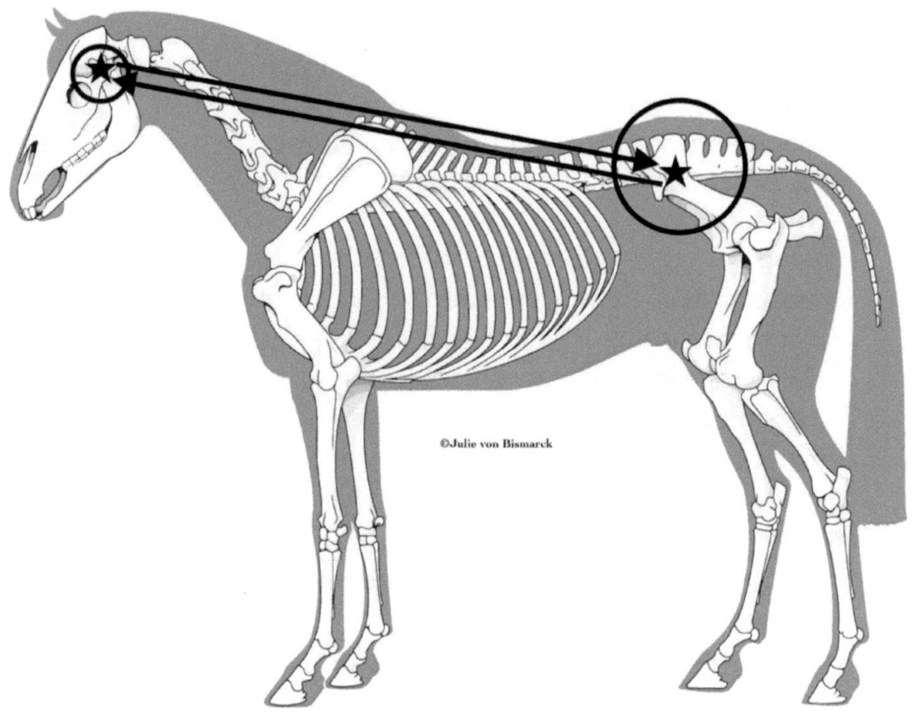

Fig. 20: The connection between the temporomandibular joints and sacroiliac joints.

In a sense, this is like a wave that originates with the hind hoof pushing off from the ground and from there spreads via the hind leg, stifle and hip and is then transferred via the iliac crest to the sacrum, from where it continues via the lumbar and thoracic spine, the cervical spine and poll/TMJs, finally arriving at the horse's mouth (Fig. 22).

Some of you may have learned to ride under the old guidelines, and if so you'll know the rule that you can only collect impulsion with the hand if you've first generated it in the hindquarters.
The old riding masters may not have known about the connection between TMJ and pelvis, but they were perfectly aware that the rider's hand, i.e. the action of the rein on the bit/lower jaw, can override the horse's hindquarters and interrupt the wave-like motion of thrust flowing through its body.

In a horse with a blocked sacroiliac joint, this thrust and impulsion never reaches the spine at all.
A blockage of one or both sacroiliac joints interrupts this transmission of impulsion and thrust before it leaves the pelvis.

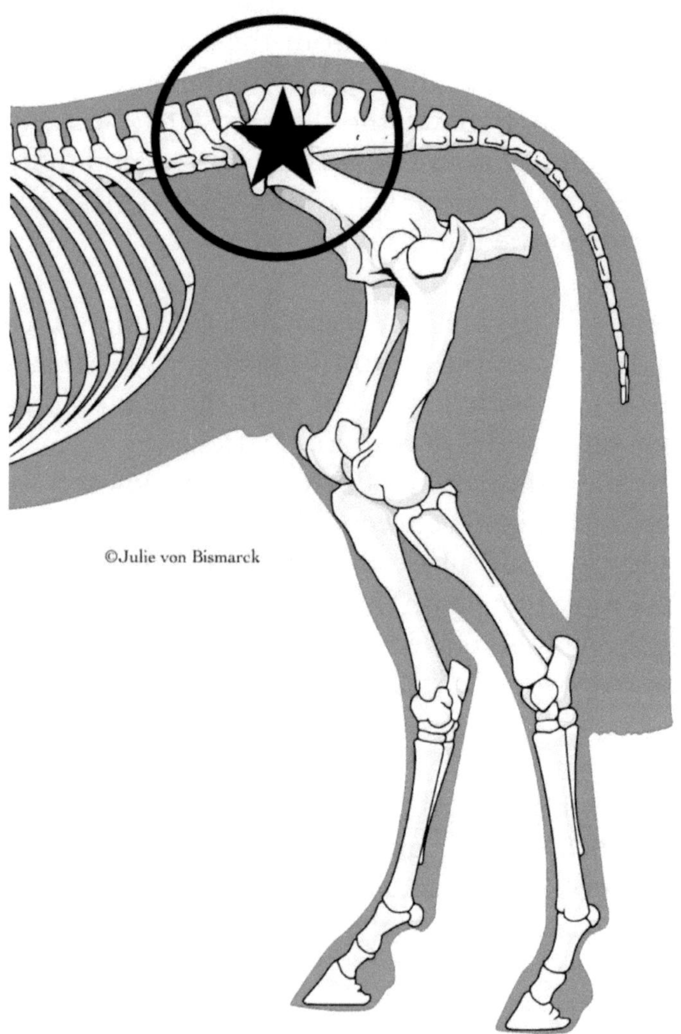

Fig. 21: The sacroiliac joint.

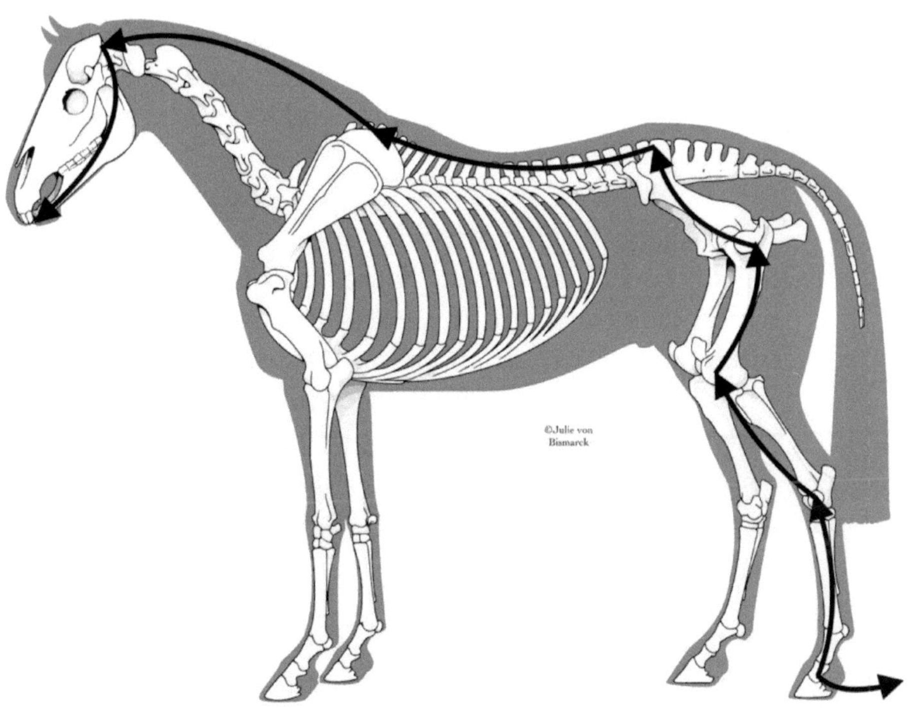

Fig. 22: The thrust wave: from hind hoof to mouth.

Lack of suppleness, resistance when stepping on the hind leg, movement disorders, lameness and chronic inflammation in the sacroiliac joint(s) are just some of the consequences of restricted mobility in these joints.

Typically, the lameness may first appear to be of unclear origin, then obviously affect one hind leg and, if not treated successfully, lead to conditions of the diagonal foreleg.

A blockage in the sacroiliac joint also leads very quickly to a compensatory blockage of the hip joint, which, due to weight-relieving (see also Chapter 7), often leads to strain in the stifle and over-compensation of the hock and, if it persists, often ends by overstraining the suspensory ligament.
I have seen many cases of inflamed suspensory ligaments in the hind leg that apparently originated in a run-of-the-mill blockage of the TMJ.

Sometimes, conversely, a horse that has slipped on its back end – an event dismissed as unimportant because the horse doesn't seem to have hurt itself – suddenly begins to resist all contact, stiffen up and rear, and develop problems with its teeth, such as hooks and uneven wear.

In this case the untreated blockage of the sacroiliac joint has affected the TMJ – i.e. the other way round.

So the lesson is this:
If a horse is found to have a blockage of one or both
TMJs, the sacroiliac joints must always be examined
too.
If a horse is found to have a blockage of one or both
sacroiliac joints, the TMJs must always be examined
too.

Similarly, the TMJs and sacroiliac joints should be
examined for conditions or blockages if a horse
repeatedly shows "non-round" movements of the
hindquarters, resists bit contact and refuses to
become supple.

Keep reminding yourself of the exercises we did
earlier. The movements in the TMJ may be small,
like those in the sacroiliac joint, but they are
essential for a natural range of motion.
And this is the only thing that can prevent pain,
strain, over-exertion and wear and tear in the horse.

Good to know:

Blockages or conditions of the TMJs, like those in so many other parts of the body, often go unnoticed.

The rider puts the horse's resistance (due to pain and/or mechanical restrictions of movement) down to "unrideability" and straps on "auxiliary reins" that are intended to help matters, but only end up making the horse's suffering even worse.

So here's a tip:

In horses that show recurring blockages of one or both sacroiliac joints, uneven wear on their teeth, clear resistance to the bit and contact, or recurring restricted mobility of the lower jaw, it is essential to get both TMJs checked by a vet in order to rule out any underlying conditions such as arthritis or inflammation.

Chapter 6

The poll and sacrum – why a blockage in the poll extends as far as the pelvis

When most people hear the word "poll", they probably think first of the connection between the skull (occipital bone) and the first cervical vertebra (atlas). But it also includes the connection between the first and second cervical vertebrae (axis).

Part of this second cervical vertebra extends into the first, and the term "poll fracture" often means a fracture of this piece of bone or "process".

Because the poll is not a single joint, this structure in the horse is often referred to as the "upper cervical joints" or "head joints" (Fig. 23).

The movements that should be possible in the poll are:

- nodding movements between the first cervical vertebra and the occipital bone, or "yes joint";
- and rotating movements between the second cervical vertebra and the first cervical vertebra, or "no joint" (Fig. 24).

The junction between the first and second cervical vertebrae is the only place where "flexion" can take place in the horse, and only if the first cervical vertebra can move freely and is not blocked in one direction.

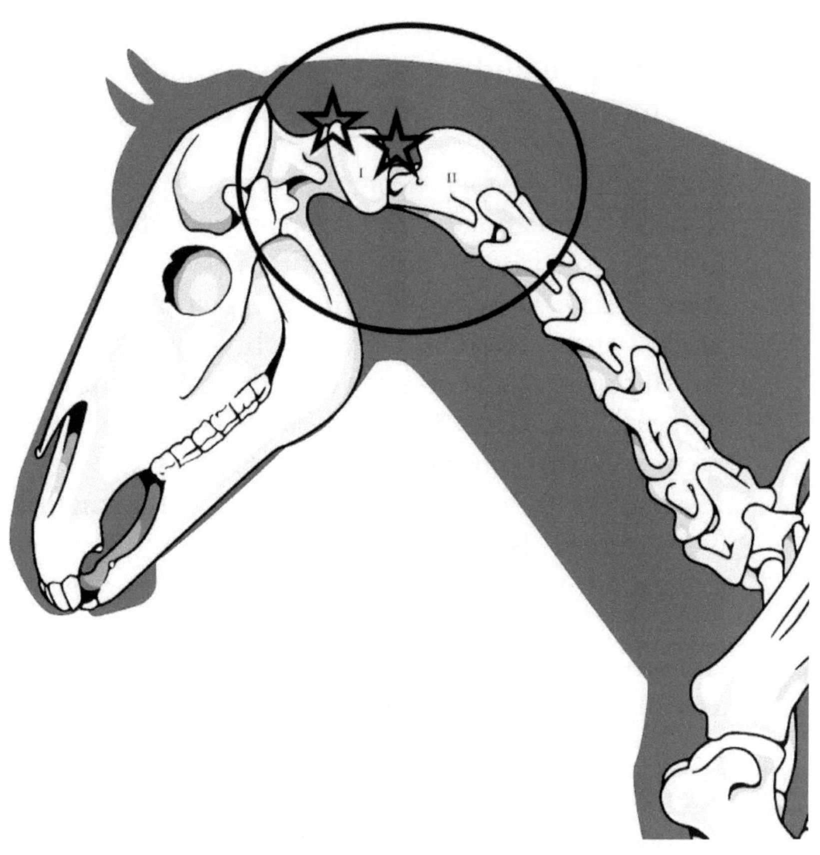

Fig. 23: The poll of the horse. Joint 1: Between occipital bone and first cervical vertebra; joint 2: Between first and second cervical vertebrae.

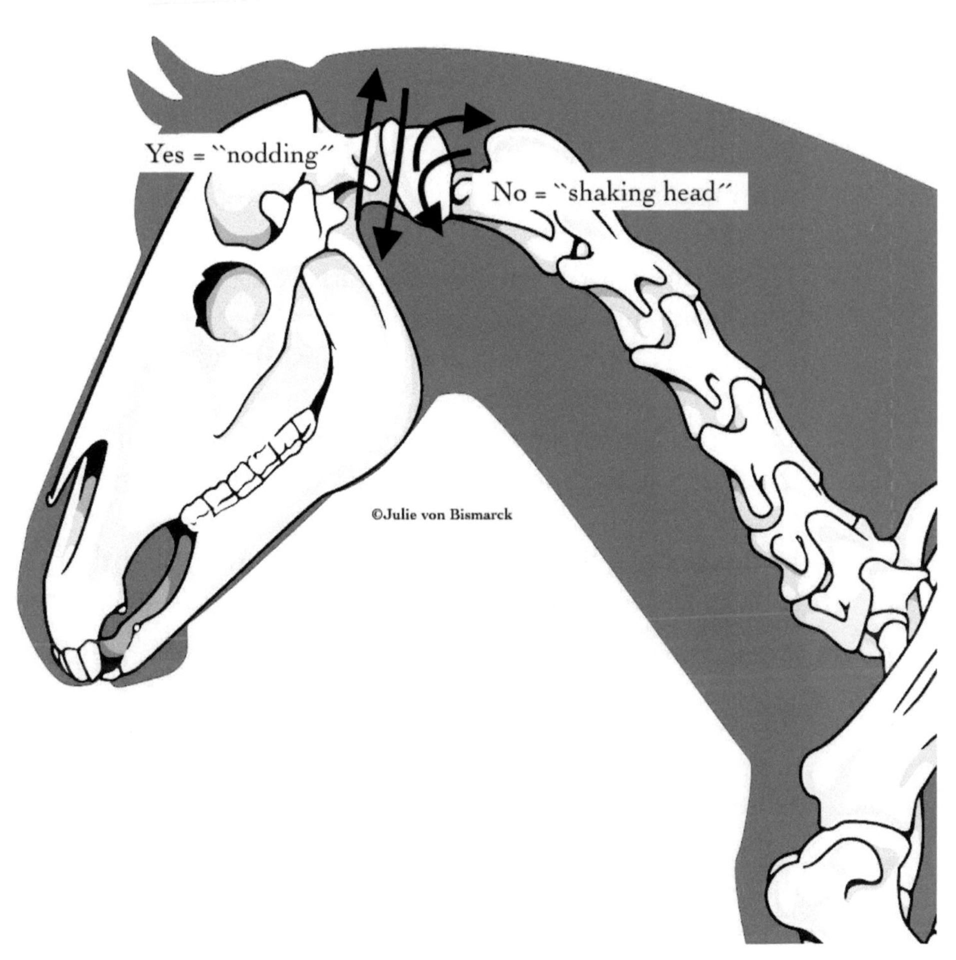

Fig. 24: Movements in the head joints.

If this is the case, the space between the second cervical vertebra and the atlas wing on the side to which the horse is flexed becomes too narrow and the horse tilts its head. One reason why riding with an "open" poll is so important is that mobility in the head joints should not be impaired.
Riding a horse tightly puts considerable pressure on the poll and, of course, on the process that extends from the second cervical vertebra into the first.

This is one reason why you should always make sure your horse has an open poll when riding.
The term "open poll" is often misunderstood, so let's put it another way:
The horse's nostrils should be the foremost point of the horse at all times; this is when you have an open poll.
In the vertical direction, the nostrils are only slightly further forward, but they are still the foremost point of the horse.

As Figure 23 shows, the poll region is very unprotected. Even seemingly minor traumas, such as the use of draw-reins, riding with a hard hand, the horse throwing itself backwards into the halter, or a thin rope halter digging in or applying localised pressure, are enough to cause damage.

Nuchal bursitis (swellings in the poll area) is the best-known consequence of this type of trauma, but other consequences we often see include recurring, hard-to-treat blockages, persistent "twisting" of the atlas, which leaves one wing slightly lower than the other and is the main cause of tilting in the poll, and very painful, acute inflammation of the neck ligament and underlying bursa.

It's important to know this so you do everything you can to protect this area from any kind of pressure or trauma.

The poll has direct connections to the following structures:

1. The temporomandibular joints (TMJs)

As you'll remember, the tension from immobile TMJs (clenched-teeth exercises) can be felt in the neck and the head joints. Blockages or conditions of the TMJs always lead to a blockage in the poll. Inversely, a blocked first cervical vertebra can also affect the TMJ, although this is less common.

Tip:
A recurring blockage in the poll accompanied by a TMJ blockage almost always points to a condition of the teeth, i.e. hooks, waves or other abnormalities in the horse's dentition.

If your horse has a recurring tension/blockage in the poll accompanied by a blockage of the TMJ, you should definitely get its teeth checked by a specialist.

2. The other cervical vertebrae

This is important because the other cervical vertebrae are the first to compensate for the resulting loss of movement if the poll doesn't move correctly.

3. The sacrum

A blockage in the poll is always quick to affect the sacrum, and vice versa (Fig. 25). As we know, here at the sacrum is where the ilium wings transmit the thrust and propulsion from the hindquarters to the spine.
If the sacrum itself is immobile, the wave of movement cannot be transmitted further up towards the head to the lumbar spine.

If the sacrum is blocked downwards, the tail often sticks out, the croup seems flatter and the horse can't tilt its pelvis, so it can't step under the centre of gravity.

As we'll see in more detail in Chapter 10, this also affects the tension in the nuchal-spinal ligament, which enables the horse to carry its back without undue effort. For this arrangement to work properly, one condition is that the pelvis has to be tilted. More on this later, but at this point I'll just say:

A blocked sacrum is one of the issues that can

contribute to "load-bearing burnout".

If the sacrum is blocked in the opposite direction, i.e. upwards, the pelvis can't tilt to the full extent, which means for example that the horse can't stretch out the hind legs when jumping an obstacle.

In this way, a poll blockage can be responsible for the horse not collecting under the centre of gravity or for hindquarter faults in jumping.

If the sacrum is blocked, mobility in the sacroiliac joints soon decreases too (with the above consequences) and the transition to the last lumbar vertebra becomes blocked.
Inflammation in the lumbar muscles is often the result.

For completeness, I should also mention that the inverse is of course possible and a blockage of the sacrum can block the poll.
Any treatment of the poll should therefore be accompanied by treatment of the sacrum and vice versa if a lasting improvement is to be seen.

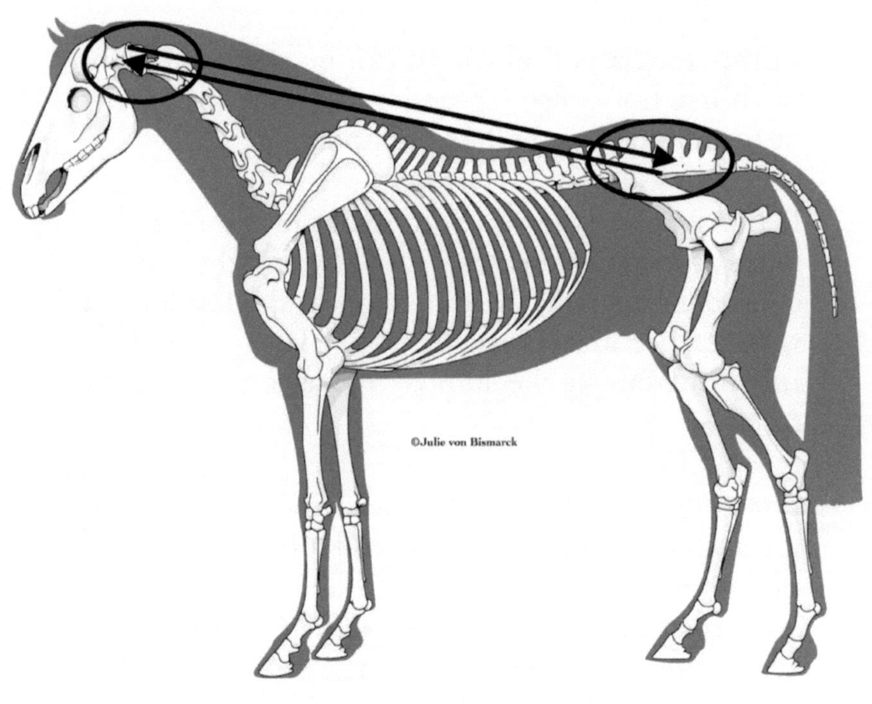

Fig. 25: The connection between poll and sacrum.

But the poll also has another connection, namely to:

4. The lower forelegs

Conditions or injuries of the fetlock head and below (i.e. down to and including the hoof and its structures) are almost always accompanied by a blockage in the poll (Fig. 26).
Recurring poll blockages may be diagnostic for unrecognised conditions of the same-side lower foreleg.
The most common of these are conditions of the hoof, such as inflammation of the hoof corium, or conditions of the navicular bone or low ringbone. But the high ringbone can be affected too, together with the fetlock joint and its ligaments and the sesamoid apparatus.
Affected horses often tend to stumble, tilt their heads, and lift their heads, going against the reins, when the affected leg is on the inside.
In this case, riders or owners usually notice that the horse is sensitive to grooming in the poll area on the affected side.

If a horse suffers from such recurring tension or blockages in the poll, it makes sense to carry out an examination of its forehand by means of flexion tests, X-rays, ultrasound and further diagnostic measures.

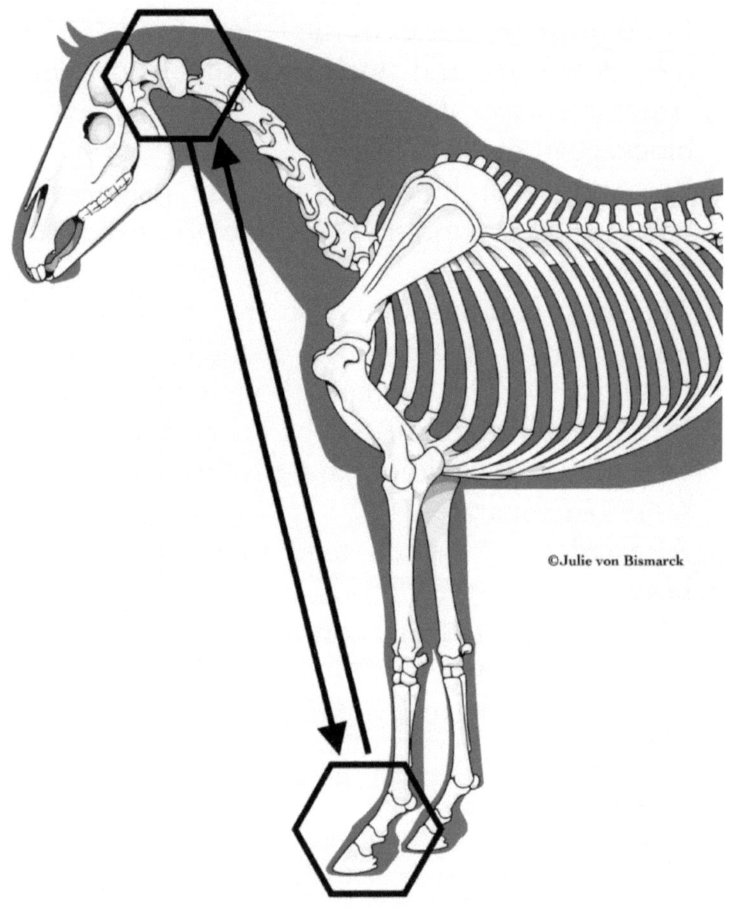

Fig. 26: Connection between the poll and conditions of the front feet, fetlock head and below.

As ever, I don't rule out the possibility that the connection might be the other way round.

In other words: if a condition of the forehand can trigger a poll blockage, it's not out of the question that a poll blockage could also lead to a condition of the forehand.

A single use of one of the FEI "training methods" mentioned earlier, for example, can reset the horse's ability to collect to zero (with this in mind, take another look at pictures of modern dressage competitions), encourage jumping faults, cause chronic inflammation in the poll and sacroiliac joints, and promote conditions of the hoof and lower foreleg joints, as well as suspensory ligament damage in the hindquarters.

At this point I would like to mention blockages in other parts of the cervical spine.

Blockages or conditions of the cervical vertebrae are very common in modern horses. We have already discussed those of the uppermost cervical vertebrae. The other most common ones are:

Single or serial blockages between C2 and C4, chronic inflammation here and in the C6/C7 area, blockages of C6/C7/Th1, malformations of the lower cervical vertebrae (C5–C7), narrowing of the spinal canal and bony growths.

The causes are subject to speculation, but personally I see a connection between riding with constraint/pressure and blockages/conditions of the cervical spine, and between the new breeding goals (aiming for two-year-olds that look like adults) and an abnormal range of motion. This shift in horse breeding has serious adverse effects on the horse.

The horses of the past, with their long, straight but unimpressive movements, lived to a grand old age with proper schooling and riding, and remained in full use (at least on our farm) until the age of twenty-five or older.

Today, many horses are lucky to stay healthy until the age of eight or nine.

As we've already seen, the reason for this is a combination of constant overwork, poor riding ability, lack of schooling and unsuitable keeping conditions, but the new breeding goals are clearly part of it too.

Many horses suffer from blockages, inflammation and bony lesions of the cervical spine, and this is not to be underestimated.

Even a slight restriction of movement in the fifth cervical vertebra, for example, can make it extremely difficult for the horse to canter; in contact, it becomes virtually impossible.

I have examined many horses that didn't canter or, if they did, could only manage a disjointed canter, or couldn't maintain the canter and immediately dropped into trot at the turn. They all had a blockage in the C5 area. After removing the restriction, these problems disappeared.

Chronic inflammation and bony growths in the cervical spine area can lead to neurological disorders and even ataxia (lack of coordination).

Riding a horse with such a condition of the cervical spine can be life-threatening, depending on the type and severity of the lesion, as falls cannot be ruled out. Quite apart from the fact that it inflicts considerable pain on the horse.

If a horse has recurring blockages in the cervical spine, I would recommend detailed diagnostic imaging in a specialist equine clinic.

It is vitally important to find out if there is a more serious underlying cause.

Blockages of the 6th and 7th cervical vertebrae (Fig. 27) have another unusual feature: a large network of nerves that extends from the spinal cord in this area into the forelimbs. Known as the brachial plexus, it explains the following connection:

In the course of my career I have examined and treated many horses in which there was a direct connection between blockages of the 6th/7th cervical vertebra and conditions of the forehand, from the carpal joint down.

Especially where there were injuries to the flexor tendons and suspensory ligament, there were always blockages of C7 and sometimes C6.

A fact that could of course be explained by the relieving or sparing posture.

It's just that there were quite a few horses whose tendon injuries healed completely only after successful mobilisation of the cervical vertebra(e).

So there is some evidence that a blockage in this area of the cervical spine prevents a complete recovery.

A horse with a tendon injury should therefore have not only its hoof trimming looked at but also its 6th and 7th cervical vertebrae.

There are also horses in which a tendon injury seems to have been encouraged by a blockage of C6 and C7.

An example from my practice:

A horse fell heavily on its shoulder, severely overstretching its neck in the C6/C7 area. To avoid a luxation (dislocation), the brain commanded the muscles in this area to tense up, immobilising the vertebrae. The horse wasn't lame and there were no other visible injuries, so the owner assumed that no real damage had been done.

A few days later, the horse showed resistance to having its lower neck groomed, but this wasn't observed subsequently.

Difficulties in contact followed and the horse wouldn't drop its neck. Rather than investigating the cause at this point, the rider resorted to draw-reins "to help", to force the horse into the desired tight, deep neck position. So the already compromised area was further irritated and put under pressure. After a week of riding like this, the horse was noticeably lame.

The owner called the vet, who diagnosed damage to the superficial flexor tendon. The horse was given anti-inflammatories and put on box rest with ten minutes' exercise in walk once a day. An approach, by the way, that might need to be reconsidered for an animal whose whole body is designed for constant movement, so its blood circulation doesn't work properly without exercise. Tendon tissue already has an extremely poor blood supply, so it should be in our interests to improve it. It's doubtful whether total box rest contributes to this.

After two months the rider decided to resume training. Three days in, the tendon damage that was believed to have healed was back and was acute again.

So the horse was put back on box rest and the same "therapy" was resumed.

Luckily, in his research, the owner came across one of my articles in which I described the connection between tendon damage and cervical spine blockages, and he made an appointment.

The blockages were removed and the horse was allowed time to convalesce. Each day after his walk, he was taken to a small paddock with plenty of grass, where he spent the day grazing. I checked him once a week to make sure the blockages hadn't returned. Six weeks later, a follow-up ultrasound found no lasting damage to the tendon and the horse was now in training without any problems.

However, it had been assigned a different rider.

There are in fact many horses in which blockages of the cervical vertebrae have to be completely removed before the horse can recover enough for load bearing.

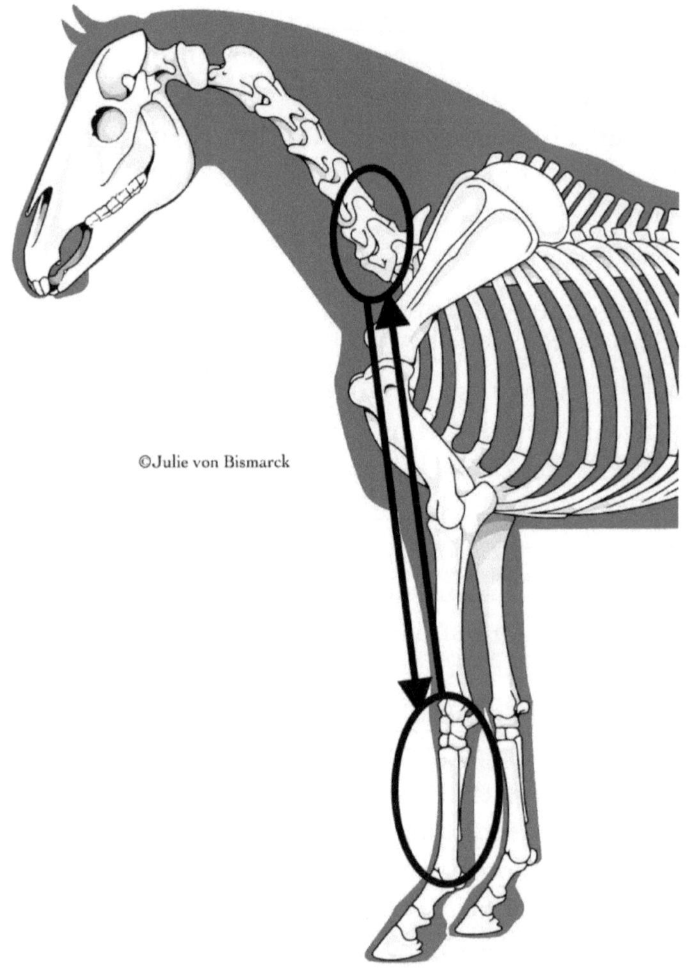

Fig. 27: The connection between C6/C7 and conditions between the carpal joint and fetlock head.

Chapter 7

The shoulder and hip joint – on "switching lameness" with no identifiable cause

As we saw in the chapter on the hyoid bone, the horse's shoulder (Fig. 28) has an unusual feature: there is no bony connection between foreleg and trunk.

The shoulder blade and humerus, and therefore the front leg, is attached to the body solely by muscles, ligaments and tissues.

This makes the mobility of shoulder and front leg very dependent on the status of the muscles involved:

If they are positively tensed and relaxed, the horse has the fullest possible range of movement and reach in the forehand.

But if they are stiff and tight, the forehand movements can soon be reduced to Shetland pony scale, even in a large horse.

Restricted movement in the shoulder area always impairs the reach in the propulsion phase and the development of thrust when the front foot takes off. It leads to tension in the transition between neck and trunk, increased stumbling, rein lameness and rider-independent lameness of the forehand.

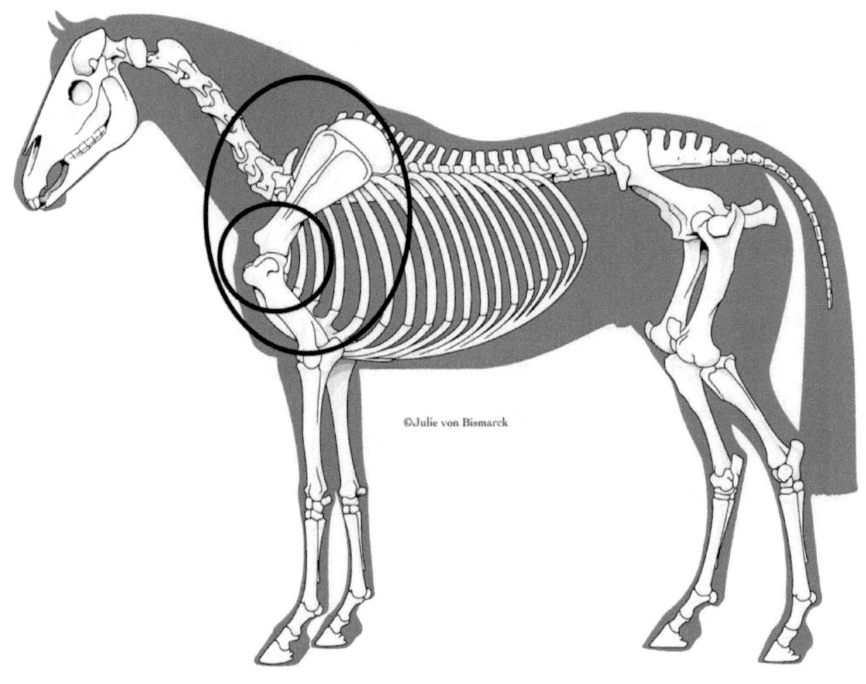

Fig. 28: The shoulder of the horse consists of the shoulder blade (scapula) and the point of shoulder. Both shoulder blade and humerus are attached to the trunk solely by muscles and ligaments, with no bony connection.

A horse with a blockage in the shoulder will also quickly develop contact problems and "resistance" to the reins, extending as far as defensive reactions such as stopping, rearing, bucking and the swallowing difficulties and possible dehydration mentioned earlier.

Because, as ever, the connection between the hyoid bone and the shoulder also works the other way round:

Restricted movement in the shoulder extends from the shoulder fascia via the shoulder hyoid muscle back to the hyoid bone in the same way as restricted movement of the hyoid bone affects the mobility of the shoulder.

Keeping these muscles in the transition between neck and trunk and in the shoulder loose and flexible is therefore vital for the reasons given above.

Of course, the shoulder joint or "point of shoulder" can also become blocked by itself, irrespective of the status of the "attachment muscles", even in a horse with exemplary shoulder/trunk musculature.

In practice, many blockages of the shoulder joint actually occur as a result of tension in these structures, often triggered by circus tricks such as the Spanish walk, forced postures such as Rollkur or blockages in the thoracic and cervical spine.

However, minor and major traumas such as falls, getting caught up in rug straps or hay nets, a harmless stumble or stepping into a hole can also lock the point of shoulder regardless of the status of the surrounding muscles.

This mainly happens in one of two positions:

Position A: In flexion, i.e. when the front leg is straight out behind (e.g. if it catches an obstacle), which means that the forward movement of the front leg, i.e. the movement forwards and upwards, is only possible to a limited extent.

In such a case, the shoulder blade is fixed in a high position and doesn't slide smoothly down and back when the leg is brought forward, and the angle in the shoulder joint, i.e. between shoulder blade and humerus, doesn't open.

Position B: In extension, i.e. when the front leg is straight out in front (e.g. in a fall, or especially if the horse steps into a hole), which means that the backward movement of the front leg, i.e. the movement backwards when bearing weight as the standing leg, is only possible to a limited extent before the foot takes off.

In such a case, the shoulder blade is fixed in a low position and doesn't slide smoothly forwards and up when the leg is brought back, and the angle in the shoulder joint, i.e. between shoulder blade and humerus, doesn't become smaller.

Common consequences of restricted movement in the shoulder joint include not only loss of reach due to muscle-related causes, as described above, but also cases of lameness that are very hard to diagnose.

Firstly, because you look in vain for any signs of swelling, heat or other external clues.

Secondly, because movement disorders differ widely in their expression, ranging from rhythm errors occurring only in extension, to a rare disorder in which the horse seems reluctant to bear weight on the leg for too long (shoulder blockage in flexion), because the flexion in the shoulder joint needed to stand on the leg during locomotion is restricted and therefore uncomfortable, through to a clear swinging-leg lameness.

Thirdly, because these lamenesses often "switch": first you think the horse is definitely lame on the left foreleg, then you think it's the right hind leg. The picture is very unclear and it is hard to determine where the origin of the lameness actually lies.

The reason for this is:

The shoulder connections extend not only to the skull/hyoid bone, but also to the hip joints (Fig. 29).

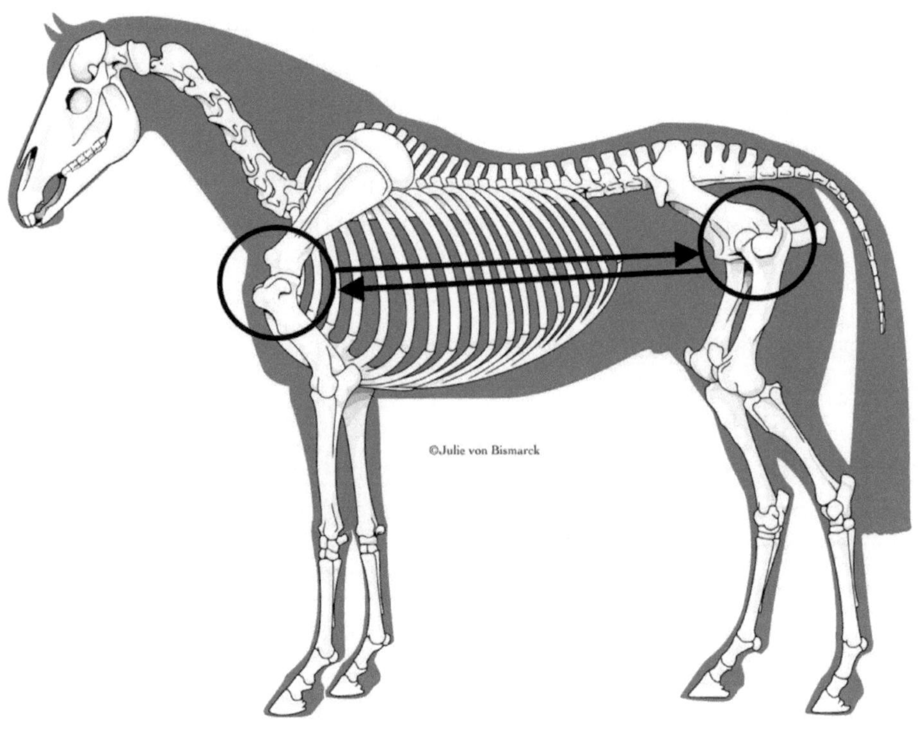

Fig. 29: The connections between shoulder joint and hip joint.

The hip joints connect the hind legs to the pelvis and are therefore the place where the thrust from the hind leg is transferred to the pelvic ring and from there to the spine.

Like the connections we have already seen between the TMJs and sacroiliac joints, and between the poll and sacrum, a connection also extends from the shoulder to the hindquarters.

The shoulder joints are the "mirror joints" of the hip joints, which means that a blockage in the left shoulder can affect the right hind leg and a blockage in the right shoulder can affect the left hind leg (and vice versa in each case).

As with all mirror joints (see "Equestrian sports - an the back of the horse") it is usually the diagonal joints that are affected.

Specifically, this means that a blockage in a shoulder joint can also restrict mobility in the hip joint and this in turn leads to movement disorders of the hindquarters.

If both the shoulder joint and the diagonally opposite hip joint are not moving correctly, it is naturally hard to tell where the lameness is coming from.

And this is why we often see "switching" lamenesses.

The hip joints also allow the small lateral movements of the hind legs, both inwards and outwards, i.e. a sideways step under the body or a

sideways step of the leg out from the body.
If this small but important movement is restricted or prevented, it has to be compensated for via the sacroiliac joints and the lumbar spine. This means that the horse moves the entire pelvic limb, not just the individual hind leg with a small, effortless movement from the hip joint.

The sacroiliac joints and lumbar spine are of course always active in all of the larger "crossing" movements as well as the lateral movements.

Physiological mobility in the hip joint is vital for fluid, effortless movement mechanics.
Restricted movement in the hip joint can lead to a painful overstraining of the muscle groups involved, including the large lumbar muscle, the smooth functioning of which plays a crucial role in the horse's movement.
If the hip joint doesn't move as it should, this muscle tenses. Since, in simple terms, it forms the connection between lumbar spine and thigh bone, i.e. the muscular attachment of the hind leg to the spine, a tense lumbar muscle often leads to major rideability issues, swellings in the lumbar region and stiffness in the back.
Horses like these bend like a plank.

Last but not least, restricted movement in the hip joint always means incorrect load bearing on the stifle joint, which can lead to real problems in the long term.

I have examined many horses in which an undetected blockage in the hip joint led to damage to the menisci and inflammation in the stifle.

I suspect that the change in limb position due to the fixed hip joint changes the loads placed on the stifle joint. In this way, a blocked hip can therefore damage the stifle if the restriction of movement persists.

This in turn can lead to blockages of the elbow (see Chapter 8) and the lumbar vertebrae, and subsequently to digestive disorders and hormonal dysfunction (see Chapter 12).

In the end, a blockage in the hip joint almost always leads to an overstraining and blockage of the same-side sacroiliac joint, because this joint has to compensate for the loss of hind leg movement in the hip joint by moving the entire pelvic limb.

If things get to this state and the horse continues to be worked as usual without removing the compensatory blockages, those in the hip joint and of course in this example the original blockage in the shoulder joint, it is not uncommon to find damage and inflammation in the sacroiliac joint and (as we saw earlier) the suspensory ligament of the affected hind leg.

Then we finally have a cause for the lameness and its location is clear too, but the original cause of the original movement disorder remains unsolved, namely: the blockage in the shoulder.

If the shoulder blockage had developed in compensation, for example due to a fixed hyoid bone, it would be essential to treat this as well.
And if the hyoid bone had become fixed due to a TMJ blockage, this too would need to be released.
If the lower neck muscles have been put under stress and tension by riding in LDR/Rollkur, causing the blockage in the shoulder joint, the entire style of riding would have to be changed in order to see a lasting improvement...

It's also important here to understand the following:

A horse can develop suspensory ligament damage in its hind leg because it has sprained a front leg. Or because its neck muscles are permanently tensed.

The horse can be lame in a hind leg because it has a shoulder blockage, or originally had a blockage of the hyoid bone.

You see, everything is connected and everything you do as a rider is important and has consequences.

And when treating a horse we always need to make sure to check all of these connections and chains down to the last possible link.
Otherwise, there is no chance of a lasting improvement.

As with almost every connection in the horse's body, the connection between shoulder joint and hip joint works both ways.
So a blockage in the hip joint soon affects the mobility of the opposite shoulder joint.

For this reason I would like to say something here about bumps to the tuber coxae or point of hip ("knocked-down hip"). Often occurring when horses are led through doorways, it is something we still see frequently and is one of the main causes of blockages in the hip joint.
Many riders, owners and yard operators assume that catching or bumping the hip in this way is harmless. It is not.

Depending on the force and angle of impact, parts of the tuber coxae may fracture, parts of the bone may splinter off and loose splinters end up in the tissue. In the worst case, fissures and fractures of the pelvis may occur.
Such severe injuries are relatively rare, but the horse will always be left with varying degrees of bruising, blockages in the pelvis and blockage and trauma of the hip joint.

This also means, by the way, that the horse will invariably be in pain – ranging from mild to severe pain, depending on the severity of the injury. Just because the horse doesn't vocalise pain and shows no external injury doesn't mean it has escaped unscathed.

In every horse I have examined or treated after this type of trauma to the point of hip, there was a blockage of the sacroiliac joint on the affected side, the affected point of hip was shifted backwards (compared to the unaffected side), the ischium was shifted inwards (compared to the unaffected side) and the hip joint was locked and painful.

In around half of these horses, the sacrum was also blocked, as was the transition between sacrum and last lumbar vertebra.
The stifle on the affected side was tender and sometimes warm (compared to the unaffected side) in every horse with a bump dating back several weeks.

This is what happens (Fig. 30):

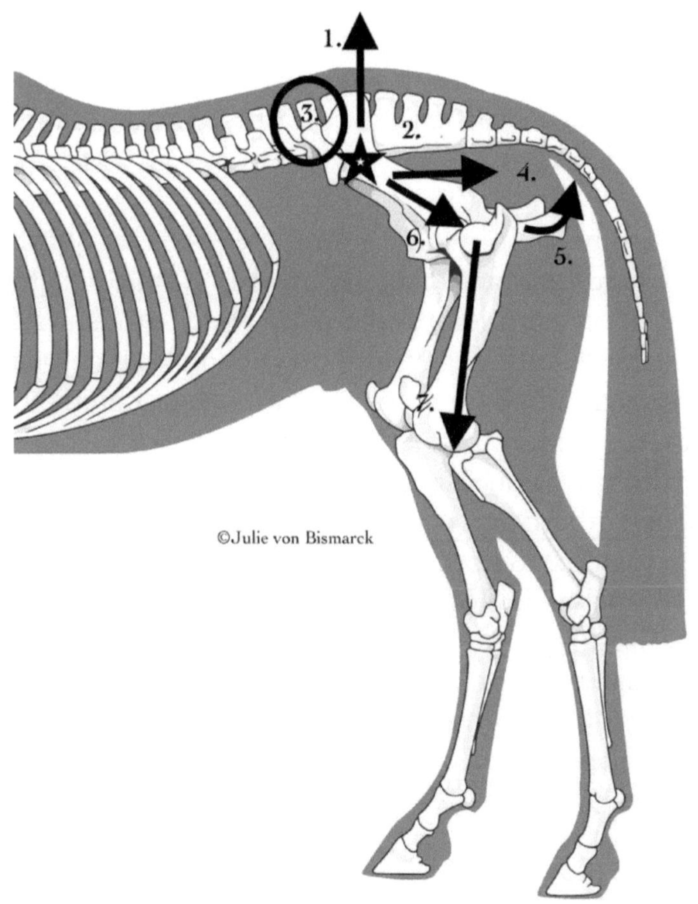

Fig. 30: Consequences of a bump to the point of hip.

The impact on the point of hip pushes the ilium backwards, trigging an upward movement of the ilium at the sacrum (in the sacroiliac joint).
To avoid major damage to muscles or ligaments, the ilium is fixed to the sacrum in this high position (blockage in the sacroiliac joint).
As a result, the hind leg feels shorter on that side, which makes it difficult for the horse to bend on the unaffected hand.

The point of hip on the affected side is shifted backwards and with it the entire pelvic ring. The hip joint is put under pressure by the ilium shifting backwards and, depending on the angle of impact, is moved outwards or inwards with the ischium and locked/fixed in this position.
By the way, you can feel that the point of buttock (ischial tuberosity) is further inwards on the affected side than on the other side.
If the pelvis is not realigned after this trauma and the blockages are not released, the muscles will eventually adapt to the incorrect position and become asymmetrical.
A permanently misaligned pelvis can be the result.

To sum up the connections discussed so far – hyoid-shoulder, TMJ-sacroiliac joint, poll-sacrum, shoulder-hip – we can state the following:

Every incidence of heavy pressure on the reins to make the horse submit, every sharp halt, every case of holding on tight to the reins, and of course every

use of painful tack (sharp bits, draw-reins) and coercive measures such as LDR/Rollkur to compensate for lack of ability and poor schooling always affects the horse's hindquarters too.
Leaving aside the psychological consequences, the physical consequences of the resulting restrictions of movement can range from acute inflammation to permanent damage to tendons, bones and joints and induce a wide variety of lamenesses of the forehand and hindquarters.

That might be good to know.

Chapter 8

The elbow and stifle – how a sprain in the forehand can lead to stifle injuries

The horse's elbow joint (Fig. 31) allows two main types of movement:
Flexion = in the forward phase of the leg, and extension = as a normal state in load bearing and at/before take-off, i.e. when the leg is brought back. In stance, the joint is held in a state of extension by special ligaments that form a passive holding device, keeping the leg in position without using a lot of energy.

The angle of flexion from this standard position can increase by approximately ninety degrees, but the elbow joint can only extend further by around ten degrees when the leg is brought back; movement in the elbow joint is very limited in this direction.
Excessive extension is therefore always countered by flexion of the shoulder joint.

Elbow joint and shoulder joint always move in exactly opposite directions (Fig. 32):
if the angle in the shoulder joint decreases (flexion), the angle increases in the elbow joint (extension) = when the leg is brought backwards, both in normal movement and in the case of accidents, e.g. catching a front leg.

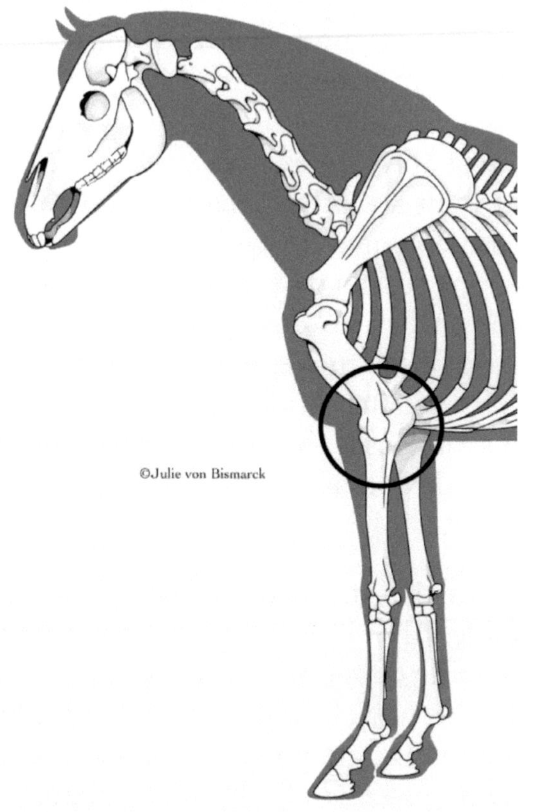

Fig. 31: The elbow joint of the horse.

If the angle in the elbow joint decreases (flexion), the angle increases in the shoulder joint (extension) = in the propulsion phase of the leg/when the leg is brought forwards, both in normal movement and in case of falls or accidents.

This is probably one reason why blockages of the shoulder joint are often accompanied by blockages of the elbow joint and vice versa.
It is also one reason why many therapists often find it difficult at first to distinguish which joint is the main cause of the movement disorder.
Assuming that the stride length is shortened, this could just as easily be due to a shoulder that is blocked in flexion as an elbow joint that is blocked in extension.

Apart from this mechanical feature connecting to the shoulder, the elbow also has a connection to the opposite stifle (Fig. 33).
On this basis, weak ligaments and slipping kneecaps, arthritis and chronic inflammation in the stifle can be treated successfully by acupuncture on the opposite elbow, and conditions of the elbow can be treated via the opposite stifle.
The other side of the coin is that an unrecognised blockage of the elbow joint can lead to problems in the stifle and a condition or blockage of the stifle can limit mobility in the opposite elbow joint.

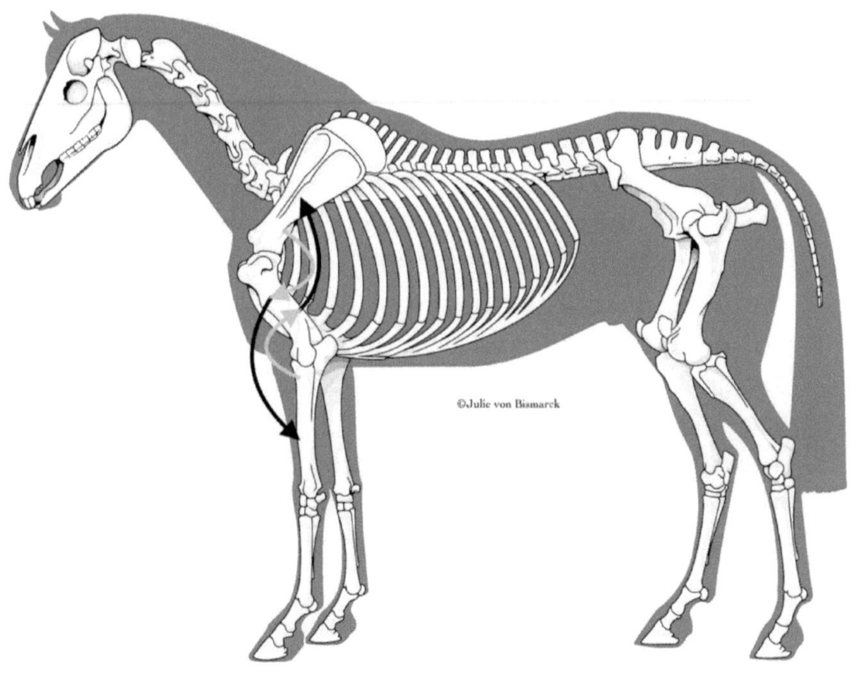

Fig. 32: The opposing directions of movement of the elbow joint and shoulder joint. If one joint extends, the other flexes.

I first came across this connection in two separate patients, and it was later confirmed in many other horses.

The first patient was a show jumper whose owners had called me in to look at a lameness that seemed to originate sometimes from the right front leg, sometimes from the left hind leg.

On examination I noticed an increased tenderness in the left stifle – and what appeared to be a much older blockage in the right elbow. I asked the owners if the lameness in the hindquarters was a recent addition, and they confirmed that. In general, the horse's stride had probably been a bit shorter in front before, but it hadn't been lame, they said.

In response to further questions, the owner could even say exactly when he first noticed this shortened stride in the forehand – after a competition where the horse had landed awkwardly in canter right after jumping a tall upright.

♦ As you probably know, horses only ever land on one front leg after a jump. Which is one reason for the various musculoskeletal conditions we see in show jumpers that are simply driven from event to event rather than getting years of rigorous suppling and systematic strengthening.

It is abundantly clear that such forces, as they affect the horse's body during take-off and landing, can only be absorbed without damage if the muscles are strong, supple and well-developed.

If this is not the case, these same forces act directly on bones, tendons and ligaments. ♦

This horse had landed awkwardly on its right front leg. My conclusion was that it had come too close to the obstacle, bringing its leg too far under the centre of gravity when landing and in the process sustaining an elbow blockage among other things.
The owner hadn't paid any attention to this because the horse didn't show any "real" lameness and there had been no heat or swelling.
The horse had been walking around for several weeks with an unnoticed blockage in the right elbow. This had caused the corresponding mirror joint, the left stifle, to compensate and become damaged too.

Later on, I saw this in many other horses:
blockages in the elbows (and the lumbar vertebrae, see Chapter 12) are leading triggers of a sudden "vulnerability" of the stifles.
All of a sudden, horses that have never had stifle issues in their lives are constantly injuring their stifle ligaments and menisci, and developing stifle weaknesses and localised inflammation.

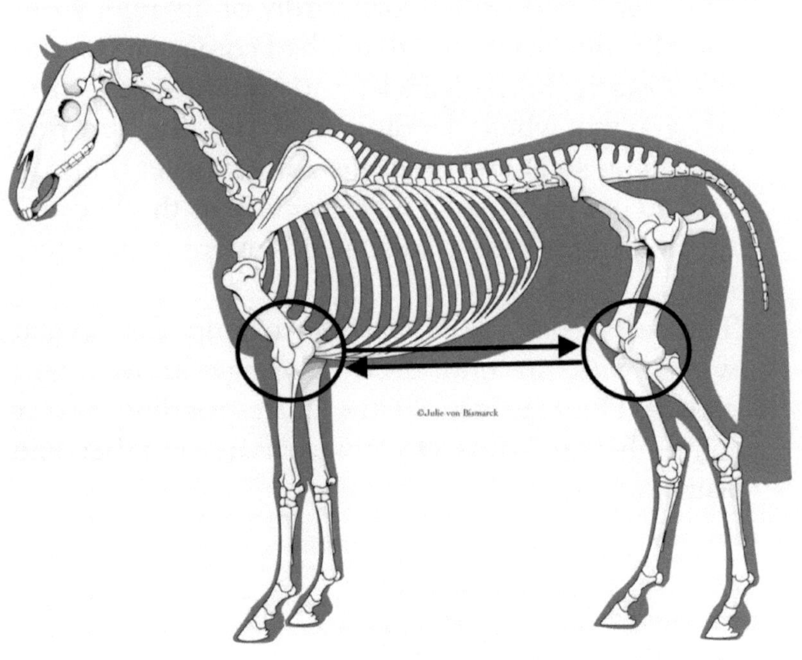

Fig. 33: The connection between elbow joint and stifle.

So it's not only a blockage in the hip joint that can affect and damage the stifle; a restriction of movement in the elbow joint can do this too.

The other patient was an eventer in which the connection had worked the other way round:

The horse had slipped on its hind while jumping an obstacle and had pulled the ligaments in its right stifle.
It received veterinary treatment immediately after the incident, followed by every suitable therapy.
Weeks later, however, the stifle had still not fully healed.

◆Note: strains, sprains, haematomas and general injuries in the stifle area are some of the longest-lasting conditions in the horse's locomotor system. It often takes months before the stifle can be fully loaded again and the horses dare to put their full weight on it. ◆

The vets had finished their treatment and said there was nothing more they could do, which was true, because from the perspective of conventional medicine the horse had run out of treatment options. So the owners had finally come to me, hoping there was something I could still do to help.

On examination, the stifle was still painful and slightly swollen, and there were blockages of the right hip joint and sacroiliac joint, as well as the left elbow joint.

This blockage in the elbow was so prominent that, if we hadn't known about the stifle injury, we'd have expected the original cause to lie clearly in the front left leg.

The mobility in the joint was so limited that the horse's stride with its left front leg was already several centimetres shorter than with its right. The elbow joint was therefore impaired in its flexion, limiting the forward motion of the leg.

The left shoulder was around two inches higher than the right.

Why?
The painful condition in the right stifle had forced the horse to adopt a relieving posture.
The mirror joint (left elbow joint) had compensated accordingly. The resulting loss of movement in the elbow joint in the direction of flexion impeded the forward movement of the left front leg.
And, as we talked about earlier, which structure compensates for a loss of movement in the elbow joint?
That's right: the shoulder.

So, in order to bring the leg forward, the horse had raised its shoulder to compensate to some extent for the loss of movement in the elbow.

Unlike other stifle blockages or injuries, restricted movement is often overlooked, especially if it is a relatively new development.
As we have seen, however, it is important to correct it as soon as possible because, once compensations for such a blockage develop, chronic injuries can be the result.

It is very important to have the horse's elbow joint checked after every fall, serious stumble or catching of an obstacle and to always check the stifle if you find a restricted range of motion in the elbow joint. And in a horse with stifle issues we should always check the elbow joint.

Chapter 9

The carpal joint and the hock – how a tiny bone can stop the horse from cantering and the role played by conditions such as spavin

The carpal joint (Fig. 34), also called the "carpus" or "knee", corresponds to the human wrist joint.
As in humans, it consists of many individual small bones, but of course it is exposed to completely different stresses.

The horse's carpal joint, like the elbow joint, is always extended when load bearing, for maximum stability.
As long as the leg is bearing weight, the carpal joint is extended.
This continues until just before the leg is lifted and resumes just before the front leg lands.
In extended trot and in canter, the carpal joint is already extended in the propulsion phase of the leg.
Other movements, such as bringing the leg forward, jumping, rolling, lying down, etc., are accompanied by flexion in the carpal joint.
This already suggests that this joint, like the elbow, allows a considerably greater range of motion in flexion than in extension.

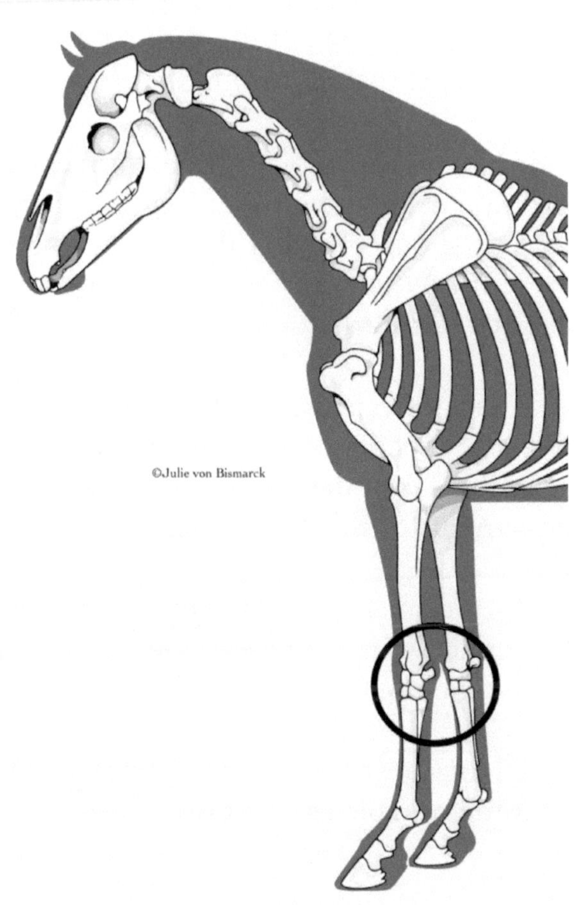

Fig. 34: The carpal joint of the horse.

To prevent over-flexion, i.e. to prevent the forearm and cannon bone (and splint bones) from meeting, and to protect the extensor tendons on the front of the joint and the joint capsule from injury, there is a small bone on the back of the carpal joint:
The accessory carpal bone or Os pisiforme (Fig. 35).

This tiny, inconspicuous bone moves inwards almost imperceptibly when the leg is flexed, acting as a kind of shock absorber to prevent over-flexion of the joint. When the leg is extended again, it moves back outwards.

This minimal movement is extremely hard to feel, at least in my experience of teaching future equine osteopaths, as they despair at their inability to feel the movements of this tiny bone.

So it's hard to imagine the huge impact that such a small, seemingly insignificant bone and its almost imperceptible movements can have.

In fact, a blockage of this bone characterised one of the most memorable cases of my career.

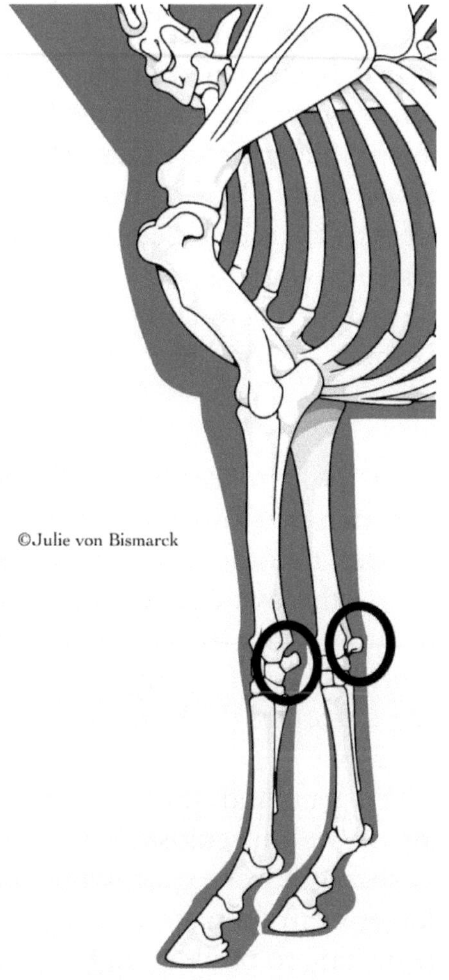

©Julie von Bismarck

Fig. 35: The accessory carpal bone or pisiform bone. An easily overlooked little bone with significant effects.

I had been called to see a very expensive horse that was showing a lameness of unclear origin and a point-blank refusal to canter.

The horse had been trailed around various clinics and had undergone magnetic resonance imaging, scintigraphies and arthroscopies of five different joints, with no findings of relevance. There was no evidence of infectious disease or parasites, no Lyme disease, nothing.

By now the owners were completely desperate and had no other option but to try "alternative medicine".

In any case, I went to see the horse and asked for him to be trotted up. This confirmed the lameness and also showed that the horse didn't seem to want to walk at all — the owner had to keep driving him on with the lunge whip to keep him in trot.

There was no chance of a canter.

Not wanting to torture the horse any longer, I began my examination.

Based on the gait and the clear and significant impairment of the musculoskeletal system and the horse's well-being, I was expecting to see the worst-ever blockages of my career.

I was even starting to think it might be easier to give the owners a list of what *hadn't* been blocked.

So I was amazed when I could find nothing at all.

This does sometimes happen with horses that have been compensating for a long time, so I inserted an acupuncture needle in a certain acupuncture point, which is usually a reliable fix, and checked again.

But – nothing. Nothing at all.
The only thing I could find was a blockage of the left accessory carpal bone.
I couldn't for the life of me imagine that this tiny thing could have caused the horse's serious problems so it was somewhat reluctantly that I started to share my findings with the owners.
I told them I would now release the blockage and then we could lunge the horse again after acupuncture, but I didn't want to give them too much hope of seeing a real improvement.

Half an hour after my treatment, the owner put the horse back on the lunge and trotted it again.
For half a lap it looked as if nothing at all had changed, but then the horse suddenly jerked its head down between its legs, jumped into the air with a squeak and raced around its transfixed owner in the most beautiful canter.
"I don't believe it!" she kept saying, "I don't believe it! That horse hasn't cantered of his own accord for fifteen months!"

I couldn't stop shaking my head either. Such a tiny bone, such a tiny movement, surely it couldn't have paralysed the whole horse?
But that was how it was. And later on I saw more cases like this.

On that particular day, after seeing this extreme reaction for the first time, I was still shaking my head in disbelief long after getting back into my car. It was one of the most impressive experiences of my career.

The owners too kept retelling the story – the odyssey around the clinics, where the vets hadn't even managed to agree on a joint, the countless bone scans, X-rays, MRIs and ultrasounds, and how in the end it had simply been the restricted movement of a tiny little bone that had put their horse out of action.

Even though it's hard to believe:

Immobility in the accessory carpal bone can cause significant lameness, it can cause horses to stop cantering, to lift and extend one leg significantly less than the other in trot (this is especially clear in extended trot), and it can cause tendonitis.

The latter doesn't heal completely until the bone is moving normally again (a common finding in racehorses, by the way).

Although blockages of the other bones in the carpal joint do occur occasionally, the accessory carpal bone is by far the most commonly affected.
However, each carpal joint also has a mirror joint, namely the diagonal hock joint (Fig. 36).

A blocked carpal joint can therefore lead to restricted movement and conditions of the hock.
And, the other way round, a condition of the hock such as spavin can also affect the carpal joint.

In a horse with a hock condition, it makes sense to have the carpal joints checked regularly, because such compensation can have serious adverse effects on the forehand flexor tendon sheaths as well as on the horse's movement.
At some point the horse will have not only arthritis in the hock, but also adhesions in the forehand tendon sheaths.

If you know what to look out for, such chains of adverse consequences can largely be avoided.

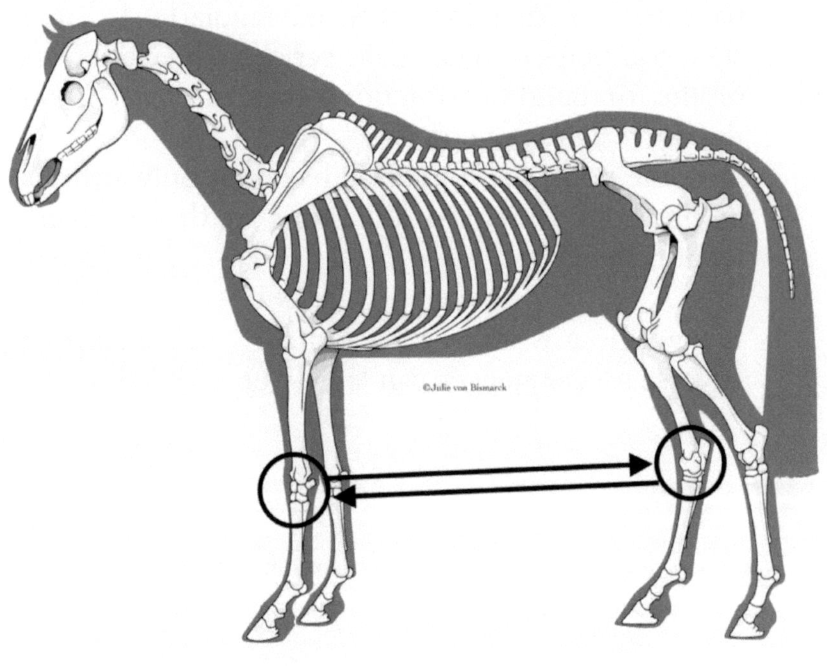

Fig. 36: The connection between carpal joint and hock.

Chapter 10

Blockages in the withers and their consequences – on chronic respiratory diseases and "resistance"

The horse's withers are formed by the long spinous processes of the 3rd to 11th thoracic vertebrae (variations are possible), i.e. the first vertebrae in the back (Fig. 37).

The withers have special importance as a supporting point between neck and back.

Here, at the start of the thoracic spine, the spinous processes face towards the tail, becoming vertical at the 14th/15th thoracic vertebrae and from there changing the direction of tilt to face the horse's head.

At the sacrum, the spinous processes start to face backwards again (Fig. 38).

These changes in direction of tilt aid stability, but it's already clear from this that such stability can only function in conjunction with certain natural patterns of movement.

A lay person looking at the horse's spine would say: "What, and then you put your full weight on the exact spot where the spine sags? No wonder horses are always in pain...".

And they'd be right.

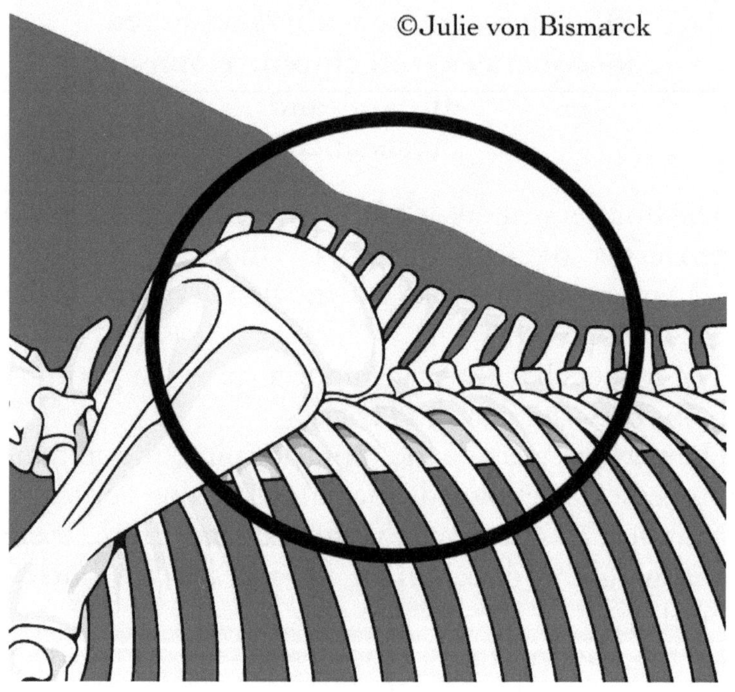

Fig. 37: The withers of the horse.

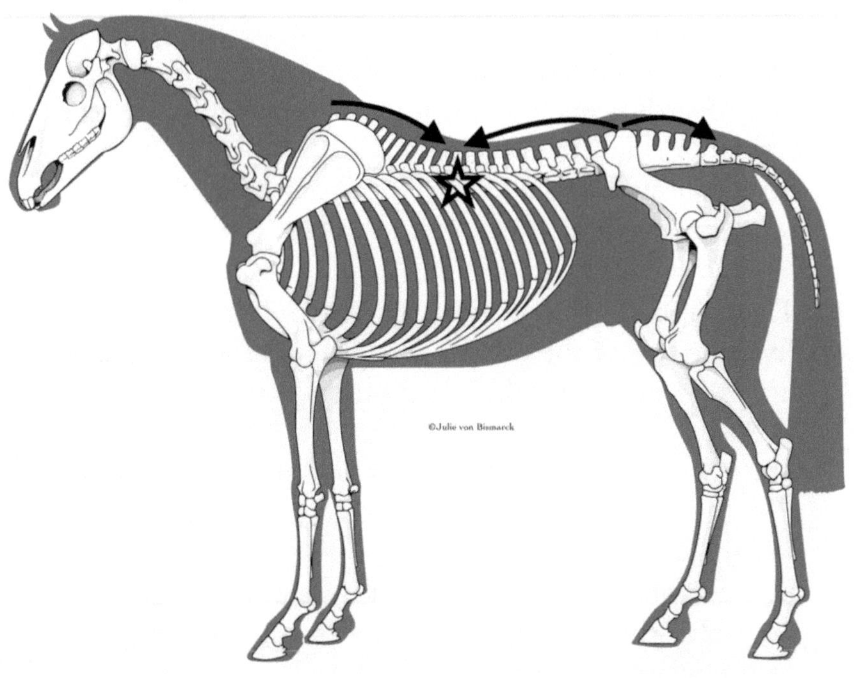

Fig. 38: Directions of tilt of the spinous processes in the spinal column.

It's true that the individual vertebrae are all interconnected by strong ligaments and deep muscles, but the combined weight of the horse's organs suspended from the spine pulls the spine downwards – even without the additional weight of a rider.
So even without a rider, the horse's back has a tendency to dip.

The empty digestive tract alone accounts for around five percent of the horse's body weight; when full, it holds around a hundred and ninety litres of fluid on average.
Let's assume for the purposes of this example that the fluid is water, which has a low density and weighs less than other liquids.
So an average 650 kg horse with an empty digestive tract already has 220 kg pulling its spine down, due to the weight of its intestines alone.
And that's before you put a saddle or yourself on the horse's back and add to this downwards gravitational force. Plus it's only if your horse has been fasting, which is hopefully never the case! With a full digestive tract, the total weight is enormous.

As if this weren't enough, there are at least 185 individual joints in the suspension bridge that makes up the horse's spine.

Each of these joints consists of capsule, cartilage, synovial fluid and ligaments for lateral stability, and in principle can be as affected by inflammation, arthritis, ligament strains and other typical joint-related conditions as any other joint in the body.

These facts taken together are enough to make it clear that the "susceptibility potential" of this structure is significant, even without the added weight of a rider.

For precisely this reason, nature has endowed the horse with a mechanism that counteracts the force of gravity and enables it to live into a healthy and pain-free old age:

the nuchodorsal or neck-back ligament (Fig. 39).

This ligament extends from the occipital bone via the withers down to the sacrum, forming the top-line under the mane crest in the neck area; from there, parts of it (the funiculus nuchae) go off to the vertebral bodies of the cervical spine.
It is one of nature's most ingenious inventions, transforming the horse's spine into a stable, load-bearing structure:
it tractions the spine, lifts the back, separates and creates space for the vertebrae, and allows the back muscles to work and develop without having to carry the full weight of the abdomen.

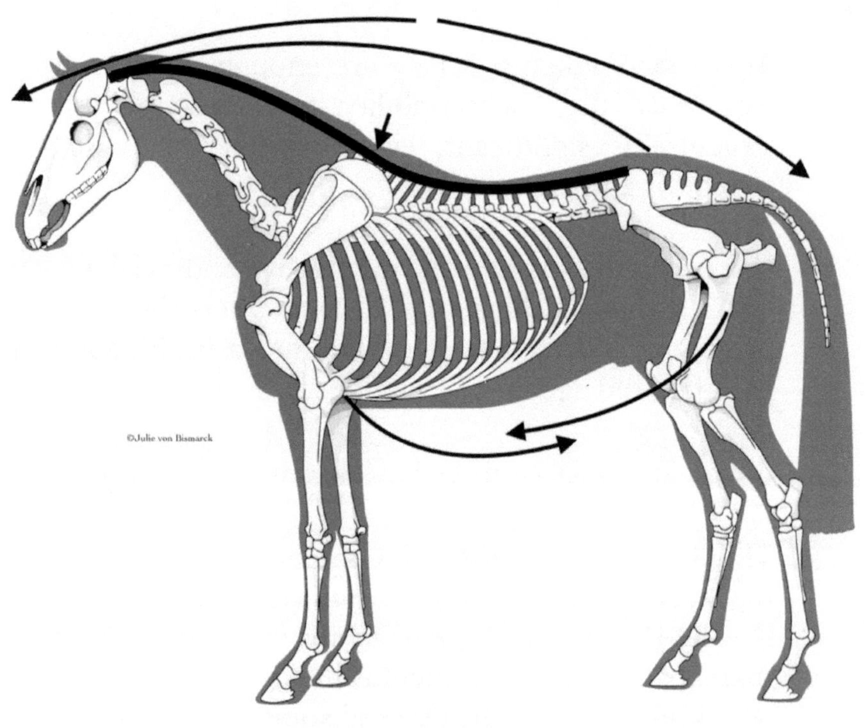

Fig. 39: The horse's nuchodorsal ligament and its tractioning function.

At the same time, when this mechanism is set in motion, the abdominal muscles are put to work:
the abdomen is lifted and the pelvis tilts (in the direction of collection), at the same time strengthening the curvature of the spine from behind, from the point of attachment to the sacrum.

"Well, that's okay then," our lay person would say now. Afraid not.

This nuchodorsal ligament mechanism is only triggered when the horse's head moves forward-downward (or is held in such a position), so the nostrils form the foremost point of the horse.
An arrangement that was cleverly devised by nature:

in the horse's physiological feeding posture (head lowered, nostrils to the fore), the back is lifted, the spinous processes of the dorsal vertebrae have space, weight and work is taken off the back muscles, and the abdominal muscles are placed under positive tension, so the weight of the internal organs is distributed with much less effort between the mechanical tensioning function of the nuchodorsal ligament and the tensing of the abdominal muscles that accompanies the lifting of the back.

To those thinking right now:
"Phew, biomechanics, boring! I thought this book was supposed to be about special connections – and why talk about this in the chapter about the withers?"
It's quite simple:
Because the withers play a significant role in the functioning of this nuchodorsal ligament structure, and therefore in keeping the back healthy and preserving the horse's carrying power.
This is essential to know for us as riders if we want to school our horses in ways that keep them healthy.

The spinous processes of the withers are the first direct point of connection between the neck ligament and the spine.
The spinous process of the 3rd thoracic vertebra forms the first real and directly linked point of attachment after the occipital bone.
From here, from the withers, the neck ligament becomes the back ligament: from here, it is attached to the spinous processes of each dorsal vertebra until it ends at the sacrum.

This implies that:

When the horse lowers its head, activating the function of the nuchodorsal ligament, this function can only be transmitted to the back if the spinous processes forming the withers fan out.
If mobility in the withers is restricted, the spinous processes cannot tilt towards the head and the neck

ligament cannot transmit its pulling and tightening function to the back ligament.

The withers are the end of the line.

This also means that the second part of the tensioning function, namely the lifting of the abdominal muscles and simultaneous tilting of the pelvis, no longer happens either.

Of course, many other blockages can prevent the back and abdomen from lifting, but here we are concerned with the function of the withers as a switching point for the nuchal ligament from neck to back.

All we need to know is this:

If a horse's back muscles are tensed, this has the same effect as when it lifts its head:

The back sinks down and the spinous processes of the withers (and all other thoracic vertebrae) move closer together.

The function of the nuchodorsal ligament is disabled, the back can't lift, the vertebrae have no space, the pelvis can't tilt, and so the hind legs can't step under the centre of gravity.

This is exactly the posture in which the high-scoring showy steps are produced in many dressage horses today. But it is a disaster for the health of the horse and its musculoskeletal system.

Blockages in the withers thus have a direct effect on the natural lifting and stabilising of the horse's back via the nuchodorsal ligament.

Correct forward-downward riding at the start and end of any training session with the horse is so important for precisely this reason:

It is the only posture in which the horse's back can swing passively and freely, the spinous processes are tilted and have space, the abdominal muscles are put under positive tension and the long back muscles can work freely because the taut nuchodorsal ligament relieves them of most of the load.

However, this only works if the nostrils are the foremost point of the horse, not the ears or the forehead, as we see everywhere nowadays!

Without this kind of real forward-downward riding, blockages of the withers occur almost automatically. Like this:

The long spinous processes are stabilised (like all of the vertebrae throughout the spinal column) by deep muscles and ligaments that keep them from touching, i.e. coming too close together, or from separating completely.
Neither ligaments nor deep muscles can be tightened voluntarily; they serve to stabilise key structures (such as joints and vertebrae), so they largely determine their own tension.
But:
If these muscles and ligaments are not mobilised regularly, and specifically as nature intended – the way a horse does in the wild for over sixteen hours

a day as it feeds with its head lowered forwards and down, trots and canters on different surfaces, uphill and downhill and through water – these deep muscles shorten or become increasingly tight and inflexible.

Once tight, they also stop the spine from stretching, as the vertebrae cannot move apart or can do so only to a limited extent.

It's like in the rest of the body:
The less you stretch and move, the stiffer you get.
And if you have back pain, you naturally avoid any movement in that area.

If we assume that it is these deep muscles, in addition to the nuchodorsal ligament, that both stabilise the horse's spine and keep it flexible, it's not surprising that so many horses today suffer from back pain.

There is no variety in their schooling, no chance to move freely and graze over large expanses, no real forward-downward movement.

Once again: as soon as any part of the head other than the nostrils forms the foremost point of the horse, the action is not truly forward-downward and the intended positive effects cannot be obtained.

In the case of the withers, as in other parts of the spine, a lack of flexibility or even a deterioration in these deep muscles can go so far that the spinous processes have little or no space left and are virtually unable to move, or may even touch.

This in turn means, in relation to the withers:

1 The transmission of impulsion and thrust (remember the wave?) that should run from the hind leg via the back to the head stops abruptly at the withers. The onwards movement towards the head is blocked.
It often looks (and from the outside feels) as if there is one horse in front and another behind; it's as if the horse is split in two.

2 The horse can no longer make full use of its nuchodorsal ligament, as this would require the withers to fan out.
As a result, the full load (internal organs, rider's weight) has to be permanently carried by the back muscles, which are not up to the task.
The spine is pulled downwards.
The abdominal muscles are permanently negatively tensed and cannot play their assisting role, which leads to "load-bearing burnout", deterioration in the back muscles and the development of other muscles that attempt to "compensate" (including parts of the croup/thigh musculature, but that's going too far for now).

Horses that are kept not only without correct forward-downward schooling, but also without all-day access to grass and natural grazing, of course suffer from the effects much sooner and more severely.

Here's what every rider should know, and it doesn't matter whether you just go for rides in the country or whether you compete:

A horse can't carry a rider without sustaining injury if it doesn't get any suppling, stretching and strengthening of the back and trunk muscles.
And, for this, tensioning of the nuchodorsal ligament is essential.

This also means:
Once the withers are locked, the best rider in the world cannot ride the horse loosely and truly through its back. This is only possible when the withers are mobile again.
Other consequences of locked withers range from "saddle scare", aversion to saddling, resistance, stopping dead in the middle of the movement (possibly with rearing), increased stumbling, tight steps in the forehand, loss of reach, refusing obstacles or flat, stiff jumping, jerking reins out of the hand, refusing collection (as already mentioned, this would require the withers to be lifted and the pelvis tilted), through to hollowing or rounding the back or even bucking during mounting.
I can't count the number of times I've been called to see horses for "resistance". In every case, examination revealed a blockage of the withers and now, after everything we've talked about, you can imagine the pain the poor horses must have been in when the riders tried to drive this "resistance" out of them...

And remember: if the withers are locked, the back won't lift. I mentioned the 185 joints that make up the horse's spine – how soon do you think inflammation, arthritis and general wear and tear will set in there if the horse can't naturally relieve the load on its back?
The causes of "resistance" should always be carefully investigated by a qualified practitioner.

Many of the riders mentioned here inflicted not only permanent back pain and chronic inflammation on their horses, but also sometimes serious, long-lasting conditions of the respiratory tract.

And this is our next crucial connection: blockages of the withers can favour conditions of both the upper airways (laryngitis, pharyngitis, sinusitis) and the lower airways (bronchitis, "cough", chronic obstructive pulmonary disease (COPD)).

In many horses I have treated for respiratory conditions, those conditions finally responded and resolved once I had released the blockage in the withers.
As any horse owner knows, it can be extremely difficult to get rid of a horse's "cough" completely.
This is not always because the horse is allergic and the cause needs to be eliminated: run-of-the-mill respiratory infections can also drag on for weeks despite medication and inhalation therapy.
This situation is not entirely without risk, because

originally harmless infections in the horse can quickly become chronic and then lead to the notorious COPD (broken wind, heaves, asthma).

This is the main reason why vets and owners rightly do their utmost to cure such respiratory conditions as quickly as possible.
And here's the rub:
Many times I've been presented with horses that had been treated for months with every remedy available – medication, antibiotics, expectorants, cortisone, tea extracts, multiple daily inhalations, salt chambers, ultrasonic nebulisers – but to no avail.
And these horses all had one thing in common: a blockage of the spinous processes in the withers.

At first I thought this blockage might have been caused by the coughing (most horses jerk their heads forward and down when they cough and I assumed that this jerky movement could block the withers), but then I found that the condition suddenly subsided once the blockage had been removed – regardless of the age of the condition.
And that means that a blockage of the withers can complicate or even prevent recovery.

As it turned out, this connection extends so far that blockages in the withers can actually promote the development of respiratory conditions.
This connection first came to my attention due to another main cause of locked withers, apart from those mentioned earlier: horse rugs.

One October, when many owners had already clipped and rugged up their horses, a lot of animals started to present with locked withers and respiratory problems such as coughing and discharge. The rugs soon emerged as a potential culprit, because in this period I had also examined many other rugged horses that didn't have locked withers or respiratory diseases.

All of the affected horses were rugged, but not all of the rugged horses were affected.

On checking the rugs of the affected horses, it turned out that they were indeed too tight and were pressing on the withers, and in each case the owners confirmed the link in time between putting on the rug and the start of the cough. Most of them added, however, that this was the first time the horse had ever had this; they'd never had any problems with rugs before.

The answers to further questions confirmed my suspicions: in each case, the horse had had a new rug that year and unfortunately it didn't fit properly (unlike the previous one).

This means that the pressure from the rug triggered a blockage in the withers, which in turn increased the horse's susceptibility to respiratory infections.

If you have a horse with chronic or recurring respiratory conditions, make sure to get its withers checked!

I have only two explanations for the connection between blockages of the withers and respiratory conditions:

1 "The Chinese connection". In traditional Chinese medicine, the point of correspondence for the lungs is located directly at the withers:

this might explain a weakening of lung function due to a restriction of the withers.

2 Stress. If we imagine what restricted movement in the withers means for the horse, i.e. the loss of free, effortless function of its natural back movements, resulting in severe pain in overloaded back muscles (and other muscle groups), the horse is quite likely to have a permanently elevated level of stress.

As we've already learned, pain is one of the main triggers of stress. And what happens when stress levels are elevated?

That's right. The immune system is suppressed.

This too might explain a connection, but of course it would apply to other diseases as well.

So, as we can see, blockages of the withers are far from harmless.

They can put the horse's health-preserving back function out of action, cause "load-bearing burnout" and inflammation in the back, and promote respiratory disease.

So let's talk some more about the most common triggers of locked withers in my experience (besides the ones already discussed):

Accidents such as overturning, which can also lead to fractures of the withers, poorly fitting saddles and circus tricks such as "bowing" (Figs. 40 and 41).

Accidents will always happen, so we have almost no control over the first of these triggers (other than not tethering horses in such a way that they panic and overturn when they break free).
But the latter two triggers are especially alarming because here the riders actually want to do something good for their horse. They naturally trust their saddler when he or she says that a saddle fits. And they also trust the advice of their "equine physio" or osteopath who shows them such exercises and explains that they'd be good for their horse.

Many of you will now be asking why you shouldn't make the horse bow, i.e. use a treat to lure its head down between its front legs, so let me explain again:

As we've seen, the withers consist of the long spinous processes of the third to eleventh thoracic vertebrae.
If you force the horse's head down to the ground between its legs – using food – and it suddenly spooks, or takes the treat and just wants to escape as fast as possible from this position in which it can't

see anything, this abrupt movement or reaction is bound to lock its first thoracic vertebra. And now take a guess at what will become rock solid when that happens?

That's right, the up to 30 cm long lever of the spinous process, and thus the withers.
Unfortunately, I've seen plenty of cases in which physios, osteopaths or chiropractors have recommended this very "exercise" to counteract "load-bearing burnout". Don't do it.
It has the opposite effect.

If you have a horse with any of the problems mentioned, make sure to have its withers checked for blockages and treated if necessary.

Crucially, the withers are one of the most difficult structures in the horse to treat – make sure you find a really capable and skilled osteopath, physio or other therapist to do this.

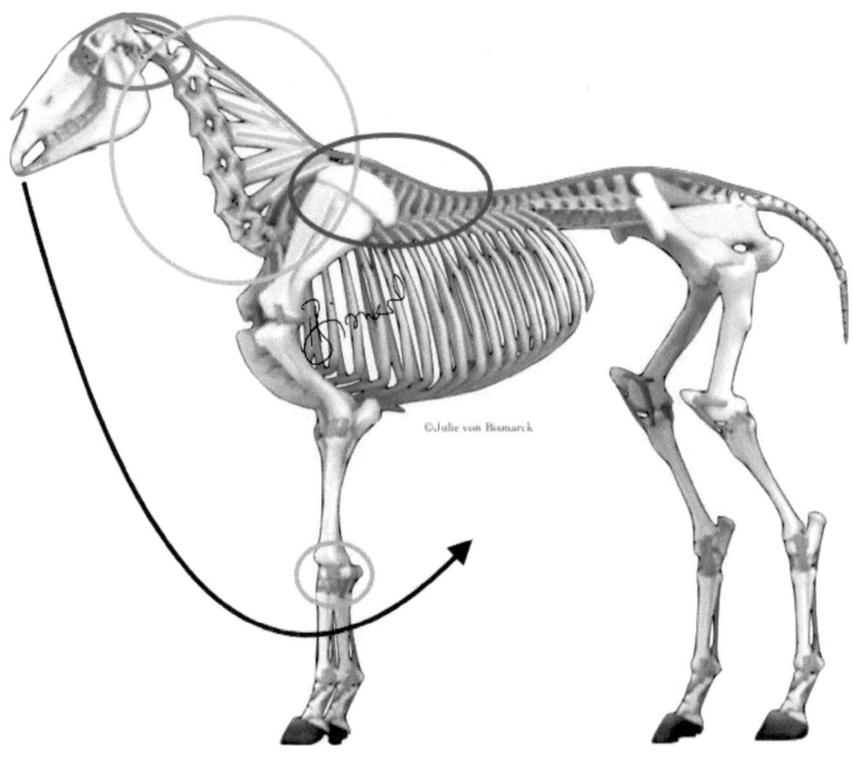

Fig. 40: This exercise aims for the same effect as riding or lunging in hyperflexion: the nuchal ligament is overstretched, as are the upper neck muscles, while the lower muscles are increasingly tensed. This leads to blockages in the poll, upper cervical vertebrae and withers.

Fig. 41: This "exercise" can contribute to "load-bearing burnout" via the resulting blockage of the withers and ensuing restricted function of the nuchodorsal ligament, and can lead to other significant impairments in the musculoskeletal system, including blockages of the accessory carpal bone.

Tip for checking a rug:

To test whether a rug fits, put it on the horse and buckle it up as normal. Now slide your hand between the withers and the rug and allow the horse to eat something from the ground. If you can still pull your hand out comfortably in this position, the rug fits. Then slide your hand between the point of shoulder and the rug and walk the horse a few steps forward; the rug should not squeeze your hand. Obviously, the neck of the rug should be wide enough but not too wide, and you should be careful not to buy a rug that slips backwards over the withers.

Chapter 11

The thoracic vertebrae and their connections – on chronic stomach conditions and colic

We've already covered a big part of the spine, but now we'll take a closer look at the thoracic vertebrae (Fig. 42).

As we know, these form the bony transition between neck and trunk. They begin in front of the shoulder blade with the first thoracic vertebra (T1). The second thoracic vertebra (T2) is hidden under the shoulder blade, T3–T11 and their spinous processes form the withers and T12–T18 is the saddle position.

Each thoracic vertebra is connected to a rib on either side. The first (usually eight) ribs on each side are firmly fused to the sternum, while the remaining (usually ten) ribs on each side end freely and are connected to each other in the costal arch (Fig. 43).

The mobility of the ribs is extremely important for normal breathing and for the horse's ability to bend. Even a single blocked rib can affect the bend and the more the rider tries to force the bend, the more the ribs block.

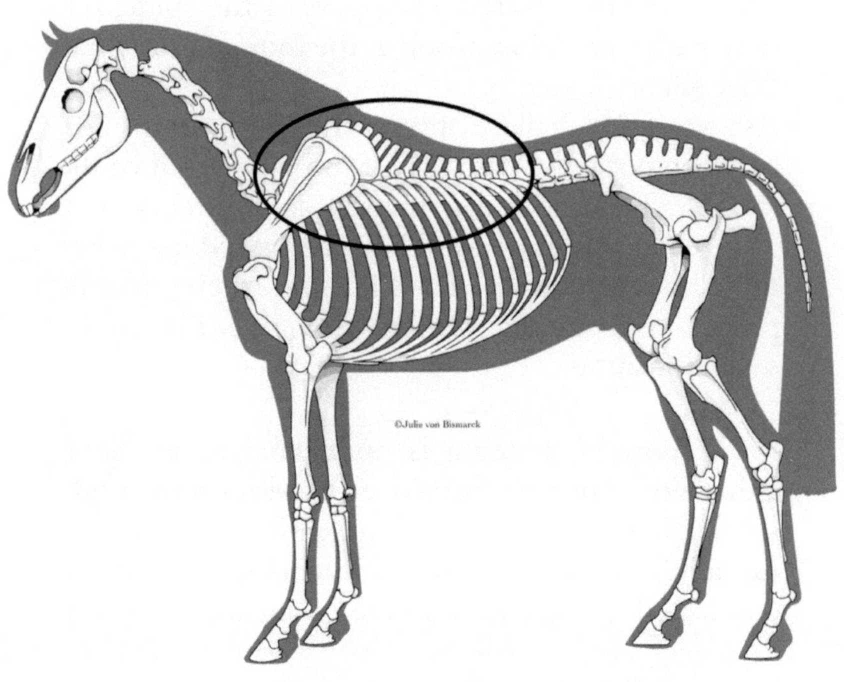

Fig. 42: The thoracic spine.

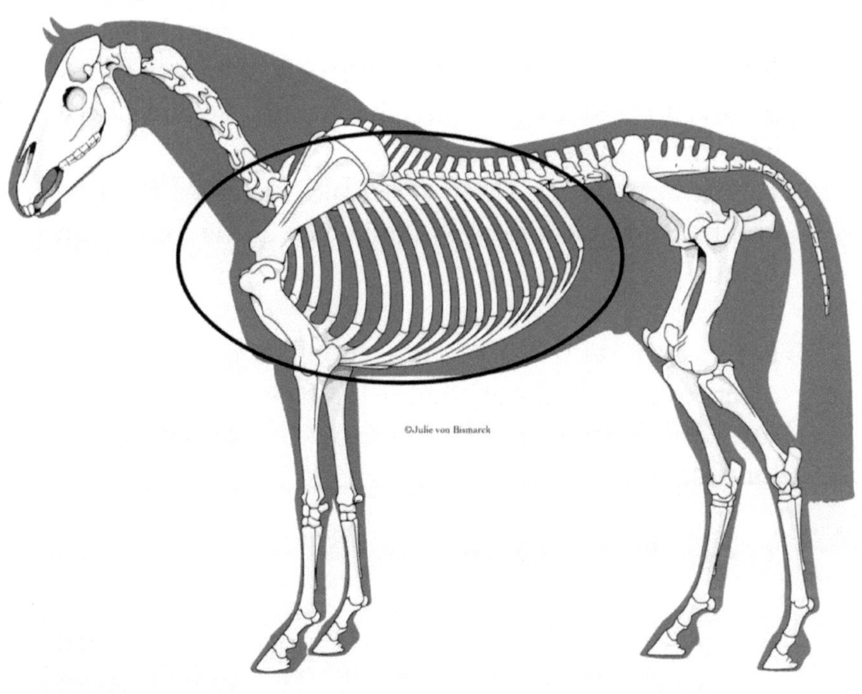

Fig. 43: The ribs.

It's not unusual to see riders riding on a very small circle for a whole hour until "the stubborn so-and-so finally allows the bend", often combined with ample spur use and tugging on the reins.

In a horse with normal sensitivity, a single stab of a spur is enough to cause blockages in several ribs. Remember how precisely a horse can target a tiny mosquito pestering its huge body – the sensitivity of its skin is amazing.

By the way, when these serial blockages of the ribs are released, it often sounds like a machine gun firing.

Let's start with an obvious challenge, one that's often overlooked but then leads to inflammation in the lumbar spine and lumbar muscles as well as the long back muscles:

The saddle position (Fig. 44).

As mentioned above, the saddle position is formed by thoracic vertebrae 12 to 18. This makes seven vertebrae, which is a very small fraction of the horse's back – depending on how long or short the horse's withers are because, as we've seen, the number of vertebrae there can vary.

The contact area for the saddle starts behind the withers and ends before the first lumbar vertebra, which is why it's so hard to find a suitable saddle for so many horses.

The saddle shouldn't press on the withers or rest on the lumbar vertebrae – unlike the thoracic vertebrae, the latter have wide lateral processes. Putting pressure on them soon leads to blockages and subsequently (because the muscles tense up) to inflammation (more on this in Chapter 12).

It is crucially important that the saddle should fit the horse first, and then the rider. (More in *Reitsport - Auf dem Rücken des Pferdes* / *"Equestrian Sports - On the horse´s back"*).

Blockages in the thoracic vertebrae, like those in the withers, usually restrict the function of the nuchodorsal ligament and prevent the abdomen/back from lifting.

Which is only logical, as we know that the back ligament is attached to each spinous process from the withers onwards.

Blockages in the thoracic vertebrae often trigger local inflammation in the back muscles around the lesion. Occasionally, this results in irritation of the spinal nerves exiting between the vertebrae. Not because the vertebra is "dislocated" and pressing on the nerve, but because a blockage is always accompanied by increased tension in the surrounding muscles, which then press on the nerve sheath, causing irritation.

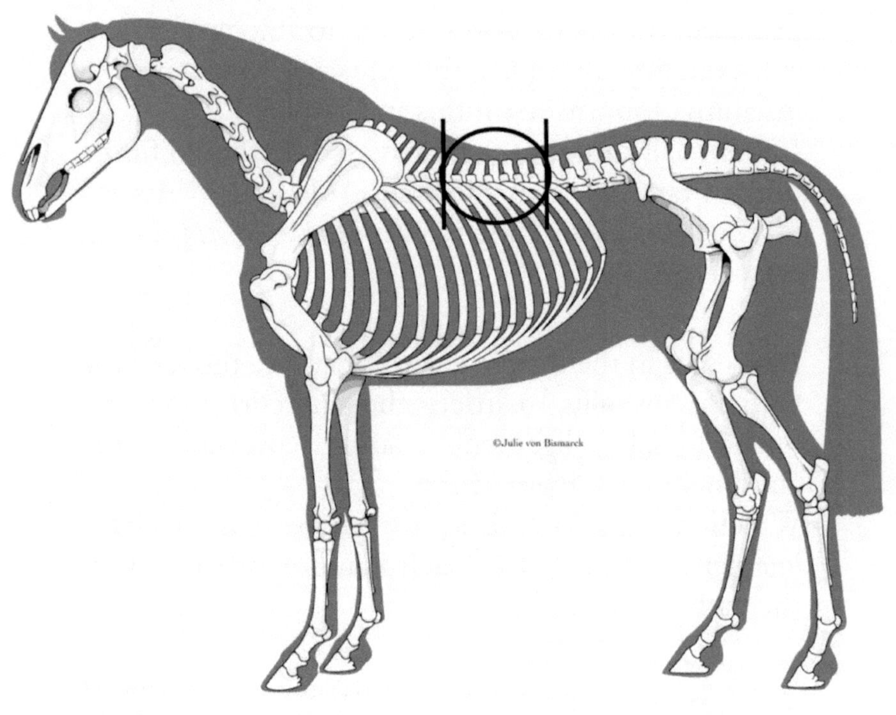

Fig. 44: The saddle position on the horse. Seeing this, it's not surprising that it's often so difficult to find a saddle that fits.

However, the most important connection in my experience is between blockages in the thoracic spine (more precisely, at T1, T12 and T18) and stomach disorders, as well as an increased tendency to colic.

Horses suffering from stomach ulcers or gastritis are often found to have recurring blockages of the first thoracic vertebra.
As a result, the entire transition between neck and trunk is often tense and tight.
A horse with a T1 blockage resulting in a stiff transition between neck and rump will no longer be keen to flex and bend, will have huge trouble achieving elevation and instead will try to keep its neck and head as low as possible (although in some cases the horse holds its head as high as possible and well above the bit).

If this horse is nevertheless forced into a posture that it finds difficult, this will cause pain. This increases the stress level, which in turn aggravates the stomach disorders. Stress is a leading cause of stomach conditions, not only in humans but also in horses.
In these cases, the 12th thoracic vertebra is usually blocked as well.
A chronic T12 blockage can lead to inflammation in the back, violent bucking and extreme resistance to saddling and girthing.

Like almost every connection in the horse, this one works both ways:

Blockages in the thoracic vertebrae can aggravate the stomach condition, while the stomach condition can trigger blockages in the thoracic vertebrae.
Stomach disorders in your horse can therefore be caused by a poorly fitting saddle, an over-heavy rider or, as mentioned earlier, riding with a hollowed back.
The other way round, an undiagnosed stomach condition (where the horse's behaviour is put down to "stubbornness", "resistance", etc.) can lead to major problems in the thoracic spine.

It's important to know that stomach conditions are not only extremely painful, but can also be accompanied by nutritional deficiencies, recurring colics, lethargy and significant impairment of the horse's performance.
Many horses have died of a colic that originated in an undiagnosed or untreated stomach condition.

A note here about feeding roughage:
Most people will have heard that long pauses in feeding can lead to stomach disorders.
This has to do with the fact that the horse produces stomach acid constantly, not only when it eats. If there is nothing to digest, i.e. if the stomach isn't full of food pulp, the acid eventually attacks the mucous membrane lining of the stomach.
The only natural buffer a horse has against its

stomach acid is saliva. However, saliva is only produced during chewing and is only expelled from the salivary glands by the actual chewing motion. This means: no chewing, no saliva, no neutralising of acid.

A horse in the wild feeds for around sixteen hours a day and specifically eats roughage, which it crushes by constant chewing which produces vast amounts of saliva, so this mechanism makes sense.

However, if horses are kept in loose-boxes or small stables (in the worst case, even without clean straw) with no access to pasture or roughage, the "empty stomach + and lack of saliva" scenario will eventually happen automatically.

These pauses in feeding are not the only trigger:

A horse kept in "active" or open group stabling with 24/7 access to roughage, can be equally prone to developing stomach ulcers. All it takes is one other horse in the group to bite it, cause it stress, chase it away from food.

I have found just as many signs of stomach problems in horses kept in "active" or open stabling, which are unable to eat in peace and have to stay on permanent alert to fend off the next attack, as I have in horses kept in loose-boxes on shavings.

Sadly, it is a common picture in today's "active" or open stables that too many horses are kept in too little space.

The horses need to be able to get out of each other's

way and have undisturbed access to roughage at all times if this method of horse keeping is to fulfil its purpose of improving horses' well-being.

In short:

Any kind of psychological stress, be it due to overwork, bickering neighbours, hustle and bustle in the stables, little or no exercise and grazing (a horse walker or tiny paddock are no substitute), pain, or even an "enemy" in the open stable, can, in my experience, lead to stomach disorders in exactly the same way as the feeding errors mentioned earlier.

The horse has a cure for psychological stress, namely feeding. When a horse is feeding, it can't be in "flight mode" at the same time.

This means that feeding is a natural way for horses to relieve tension.

Providing roughage, i.e. good-quality hay, teff and straw, is therefore an excellent way to prevent stomach conditions. Almost as good as year-round, 24-hour grazing with coarse-textured grass and roughage stations in the winter.

If a stomach condition has been detected by gastroscopy, drugs known as proton pump inhibitors can help the mucous membrane to recover. However, these drugs should be given for only as long as really needed, as they restrict the production of stomach acid, which is essential for the horse to digest its food.

This means that they are solely an urgent measure to preserve the stomach lining, not a long-term therapy.

Once the acute disorder has been cured, a "stomach protector" should be fed for a few more weeks. Stomach protectors are mostly herbal medicines or feed supplements that mechanically line or protect the mucosa, for example by producing a mucous film.

(If interested to see what these films look like, mix some flaxseed with water and leave it to swell.)

In addition, of course, the suspected or proven cause of the stomach condition must be eliminated and the horse should always be examined for blockages of T1 and T12. Because if these are not released, they can prevent recovery and lead to recurrences.

The following symptoms are often an indication of stomach conditions and blockages of T1 and T12:

- sensitivity and resistance to grooming of the (lower) neck
- resisting the saddle and girth – many geldings start to tremble on a front leg when being girthed, while mares tend to prick their ears and bite the air
- trouble picking up the front legs, horse pulls away during hoof picking or is reluctant to give the front feet, leans on the leg being picked up, starts to shake or wobble on the standing leg, buckles in the carpal joint

- long warming-up phase until the horse drops its neck
- lack of suppleness
- no impulsion over the back
- frequent yawning
- "resistance"
- girthiness or cinchiness
- general "unwillingness"

Only gastroscopy can provide a reliable diagnosis.

Of course, you needn't do a gastroscopy straight away, just because the horse is sensitive to having its neck groomed, but if this behaviour persists and the osteopath keeps finding the blockages mentioned, a gastroscopy is indicated.
Especially if one or more of the above symptoms are observed as well.
The change that takes place in horses when the blockages are released and the stomach pain stops is impressive.
They literally blossom and relax, go back to bucking and playing, and enjoy working again.

In any case, the horse should always have an adequate and ideally continuous supply of roughage, i.e. good-quality straw, hay, alfalfa hay or even dried reeds.
Silage or haylage is not roughage in the true sense and is not tolerated well by the vast majority of horses.

Blockages of the 18th thoracic vertebra also have a special feature: that there seems to be a connection between a blockage of the last thoracic vertebra and an increased tendency to colic, or recurring colics. Of course, there are many possible reasons for this, but:

In every horse that I have treated during (or immediately after) a colic, T18 was blocked.
Every time.
Which is why I can't rule out the possibility that a T18 blockage might be involved in the origins of colic.

I was especially struck by the cases in which horses hadn't had a single colic in years and then, after a new saddle, an accident, a fall, slipping on their back end, etc. – i.e. triggers for T18 blockages – suddenly got one colic after another.

T18 usually blocks together with the first lumbar vertebra (L1); this is referred to as a blockage of the thoracolumbar transition. It often happens as a result of uncontrolled slipping (sideways or with the hindquarters under the body or out backwards), or falls, or simply because the saddle contact surface is too long and leads to blockages in the first lumbar vertebra.

After successful removal of the T18 blockage and also the L1 blockage if necessary, nine out of ten horses had no recurrence of colic.

If your horse has had a colic or indeed is prone to colic, I think it is worthwhile to have these vertebrae examined, and treated if necessary.

Chapter 12

The lumbar vertebrae and their connections – faecal water, stifle weakness and reproductive impairments

In our last chapter on the connections in the horse's body, we will look at the lumbar spine (Fig. 45).

We've already seen that the shape of the vertebrae here differs from that of the thoracic vertebrae, and that they give a very high degree of stability due to their lateral processes.

This stability is especially important because this part of the spine is not stabilised by the costal arch or pelvic ring, but is freely suspended. It is also the part of the spine where the concentrated forces and thrust of the hindquarters are passed on or transmitted from the sacrum to the spine via the joint connections between the last lumbar vertebra and the sacrum.

As we also remember, the large lumbar (psoas) muscle attaches the thigh to the lumbar spine from the inside, effectively forming a muscular connection from the hind leg to the spine.

So, in addition to the connection with the sacrum, the lumbar spine is also in direct contact with the movements of the hind legs via this muscle.

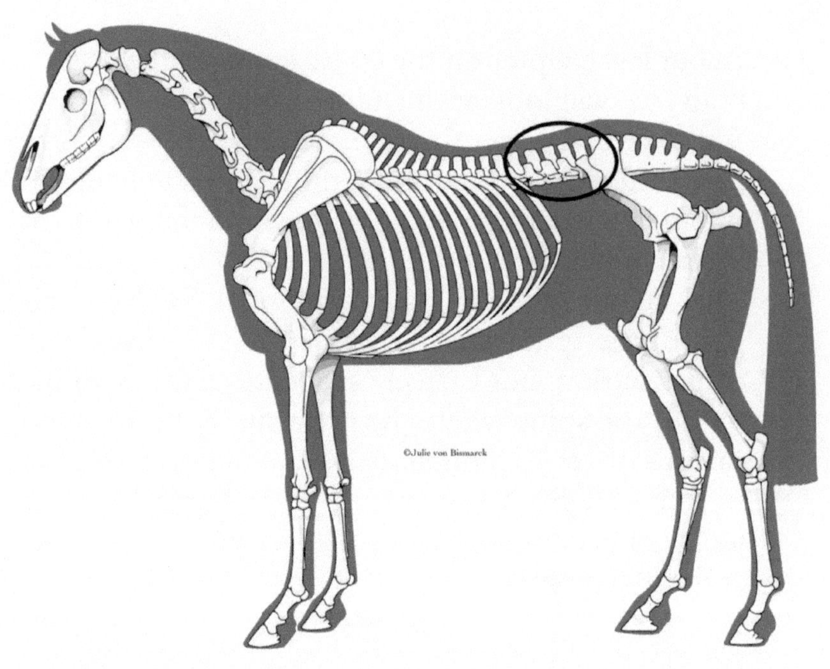

Fig. 45: The lumbar spine of the horse.

A blockage in one or more lumbar vertebrae means that our movement "wave" cannot be transmitted from the hind legs to the back.

The lumbar vertebrae also play an important role in crossing movements such as leg-yield or half-pass and in successful rolling, i.e. both halves of the body in one go without standing up in between.
Restricted mobility in this area can cause the horse to push with its hindquarters into the track and to move almost like a dog on three or four tracks; there are problems with lateral movements and horses often don't get all the way over when rolling, or don't roll at all.

Recurring blockages in the lumbar vertebrae are often connected to:

1. Conditions of the stifle (Fig. 46)

Especially if there is growth-related instability of the stifle joints – due to a luxating (slipping) or fixed patella – which is very common in modern horses between the ages of five and eight, a blockage of L3 and L5 is almost always found as well.

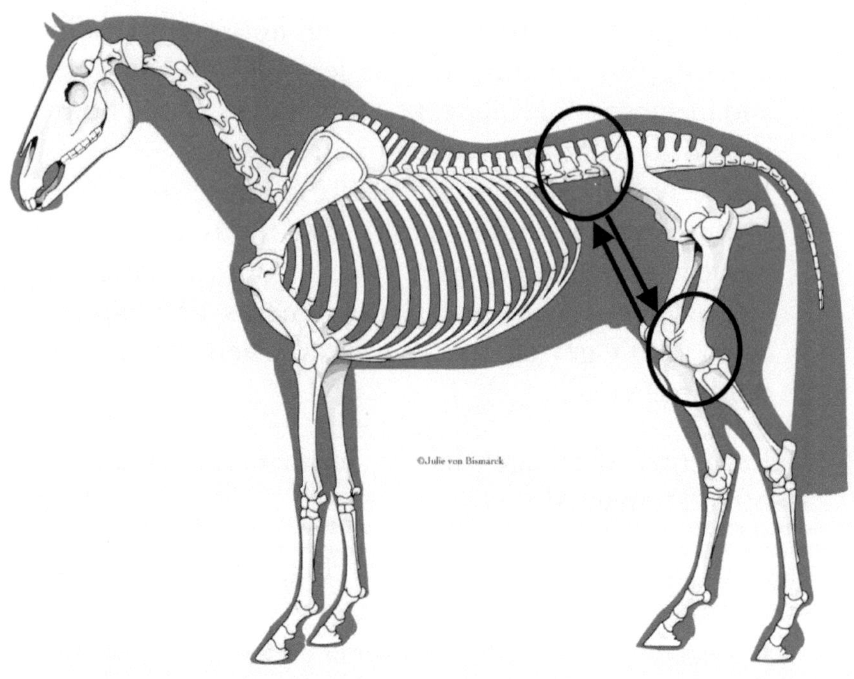

Fig. 46: The connection between the lumbar vertebrae and the stifle joints, including patella.

Instability of the patella leads to movement disorders, which are especially clear in trot, on the lunge and in tight turns when the affected leg is on the outside.

This is accompanied by a noticeable delay in the propulsion phase.

Affected horses also have serious difficulty with load bearing or collection as they are not keen to bear weight on the unstable leg.

If the leg has buckled twice under a load, horses are understandably reluctant to stand on it a third time. We also often see a sagging/buckling of the hindquarters in the transitions from canter to trot and, even more noticeably, from trot to walk.

In some cases, the patella becomes fixed. The leg appears stiff and is brought back/forward in extended position. Both versions are usually growth-related, but an experienced equine vet should be consulted to be on the safe side.

Stifle conditions due to injury, trauma or wear and tear can cause blockages of the lumbar vertebrae.

Remember the case of the eventer that sustained a long-term stifle injury after catching a leg on an obstacle. The stifle couldn't heal completely until not only the blockages in the elbow joint but also those in the lumbar spine were removed.

And in this case too, this fact means that the connection goes both ways. Not only do lumbar vertebrae become blocked as a result of pain, disease or dysfunction in the stifles; a blockage in the lumbar spine can increase the stifles' susceptibility to injury and affect the horse's recovery from conditions of the stifle.

Blockages in the lumbar spine are also connected to:

2. Digestive disturbances

The most common of these is faecal water, but there may also be connections between blockages of the lumbar vertebrae and chronic diarrhoea.
In every horse with faecal water that I have examined, there were blockages in the lumbar spine. It was usually L3 and L4 that were affected and in the vast majority of horses the faecal water was completely eliminated by simply removing the blockages.

If the upset has an internal cause, such as unsuitable feed (haylage, silage, etc.), allergies, stomach ulcers or inflammation of the gastrointestinal tract, the blockages in the lumbar vertebrae will however keep recurring until the cause has been removed.

During this time, the lumbar vertebrae should nevertheless be mobilised regularly to support recovery.
In such cases, the absence of blockages in the lumbar vertebrae can tell you whether the causes or conditions that led to the faecal water have been eliminated.

If faecal water is purely excitement-related or situational, i.e. due to the first fresh pasture grass, transport, a new stable mate, a competition, etc.) the horses have no blockages of the lumbar vertebrae.

The third connection is that between the lumbar vertebrae and:

3. Diseases or disorders of the reproductive organs and endocrine (hormone) system

I have treated and examined both mares and stallions (the mares for cysts in the ovaries or uterus or hormonal dysfunctions, and the stallions for pulled-up testicles, reluctance to mate, inflammation of the spermatic cords or other reproductive conditions), and have always found a blockage of the second, and sometimes the fifth, lumbar vertebra.
All of these dysfunctions and difficulties resolved or responded to treatment only after the blockages had been removed.
The direct nature of the connection became clear in a case that, like that of the blocked accessory carpal bone, I will never forget:

I was called to see a stallion who had pulled up his testicles, couldn't walk properly and certainly didn't want to mate.
It was mid-season and the owners were getting pretty desperate because the semen had already been sold.

Both testicles were pulled up and the horse's whole back was as stiff as a board, especially the lumbar muscles. Absolutely nothing was moving and everything seemed to be extremely painful.
The stallion wouldn't take a single step on his own and when I made him walk a few steps, I felt so sorry for him that I cut the gait assessment short.
To be honest, the horse looked as if he had an acute case of azoturia or "tying up syndrome".

When asked, the worried owners said that this had already been ruled out; the horse had been like this for four days now and they'd already had the vet out of course. The blood tests had been normal and the vet couldn't find anything else to explain these symptoms.
I suspected at least a blockage, if not a strain or sprain, in the lumbar spine and asked if anything out of the ordinary had occurred.
Yes, the owners replied, the stallion had slipped off the phantom with one hind leg during mating ten or so days ago, but it had all been pretty uneventful, no cause for concern, especially as he had mounted the phantom again immediately.

To my mind, this account explained all of the symptoms the stallion was showing.

I treated the lumbar spine and the lumbosacral junction, i.e. the transition between the last lumbar vertebra and the sacrum, and when I had finally

released L2 I said half-jokingly:
"So now we wait a couple of minutes and the testicles will be back."

It didn't take that long.
I'd hardly finished the sentence when, one after the other, the testicles reappeared and naturally resumed their proper place.
The horse snorted in great satisfaction and his back relaxed immediately.

The owners were stunned.

Let's go over what exactly had happened to the poor horse, because this applies to all trauma-related lumbar blockages and is therefore important:

As we know, the last lumbar vertebra is connected to the sacrum via several joints. The sacrum in turn connects to the pelvis and, via the hip joints, to the hind legs.
We know from the chapter on the sacroiliac joints that movements of the hind legs have a very direct effect there.
If a horse slips on one or both legs, as in the case of this stallion, the affected sacroiliac joint immediately locks to prevent more serious damage.

However, the sacroiliac joint, as its name implies, is part of the sacrum, which in turn means that a sudden standstill like this will also lock the sacrum.
In a case like this, this locking of the sacrum is immediately passed on; in less sudden situations, it

also passes on eventually to the last lumbar vertebra, which then becomes fixed too.

As we've already seen, the structure of the lumbar spine is very stable, so a blockage in a lumbar vertebra almost always affects the whole area.

This also means that if a horse has suffered a trauma like this, e.g. a slip of the hindquarters, the sacroiliac joints and lumbar vertebrae should be checked as a precaution, otherwise the horse could suddenly develop faecal water, diarrhoea or hormonal dysfunctions.

The connection between the L2 and dysfunctions of the reproductive organs or hormone metabolism may lie, as with blockages of C6 and C7 and forehand tendon disorders, in irritation of the nerve sheaths of the spinal nerves exiting in this area.
Whatever the reason, the connection has been confirmed time and again in practice in both the treatment of reproductive conditions or dysfunctions and the treatment of hormonal dysfunction.

Tip:

In mares with recurring blockages of the lumbar vertebrae, I recommend an ultrasound investigation of the reproductive organs together with blood tests to ascertain the hormone levels.
Many mares that are considered "unrideable" and "difficult" in reality simply have back pain and

suffer from hormonal fluctuations — from "premenstrual syndrome", in a sense.

An uncomfortable (too long) saddle, a seemingly harmless slip of the hindquarters, unnoticed trouble standing up in the loose-box, riding in Rollkur/LDR or without regular real forward-downward work can all lead to chronic digestive disorders or intestinal inflammation, can turn a gentle, friendly mare into a biting, kicking, squealing, bucking fury, can stop a stallion from mating and trigger symptoms similar to those of "tying up".
All because a lumbar vertebra may be blocked.

It is important to understand that a single injury, blockage, or disease of an organ can never be considered in isolation.

The connections in the horse extend so far that I could have written this book as a single chapter — ranging from the consequences of poor training to the fight or flight instinct to the hyoid bone, the TMJs and sacroiliac joints, the poll and sacrum, the shoulder, the hyoid and hip, the elbow and stifle, the carpal joint and hock, the withers and nuchodorsal ligament, the thoracic vertebrae and stomach conditions, the lumbar vertebrae and stifle problems, through to reproductive dysfunction — but all of that would have been far too complicated and confusing.

But just as an example of how everything might fit together:

A bad rider reins his horse in tightly because he's afraid of losing control, the horse tries in vain to lift its head to assess the risk, it gets scared and stressed and locks its hyoid bone, TMJ and poll as well as C3 and C4.

Then the shoulder locks due to the fixed hyoid bone, which also obstructs the act of swallowing. At the same time, the TMJ blockage restricts the chewing motion, leading in turn to reduced saliva production. Most of the saliva that *is* produced is not swallowed (due to the fixed hyoid), so the horse develops stomach pain.

This blocks the thoracic spine, which in turn leads to compensation and fixes the withers.

The stress level rises because the back muscles are now overloaded, as the nuchodorsal ligament cannot fulfil its function due to the blockages in the withers and thoracic spine.

The horse develops a respiratory condition (due to the blocked withers and suppressed immune system).

The fixed TMJ leads to dental problems, meanwhile the sacroiliac joints and sacrum are also blocked, and with them the lumbar spine.

Now the horse develops faecal water and tense, painful lumbar muscles.

The hip joint locks, straining and damaging the stifle, which is already weakened by the blockage in the lumbar vertebrae. The elbow now locks as well, partly due to the locking of the shoulder, and partly in response to the pain in the stifle.

The restricted movement in the elbow leads to a fixing of the accessory carpal bone, i.e. a blockage in the carpal joint, which immediately transmits to the hock, where it leads to wear and tear and inflammation. Due to the persistent blockage of the sacroiliac joint, the fetlock suspensory ligament becomes irritated too.

Last but not least, due to the now stiff transition between neck and trunk, the last two cervical vertebrae become locked. This, combined with the blocked carpal joint and compensation for the sore opposite hock, finally leads to severe damage to the superficial flexor tendon in the front leg...

And this chain of events could be taken even further.

On the final page of this book is a diagram in which I had started to list all the effects or connections that I have found during my career just for blockages of the TMJ.

I had to stop eventually because the computer program crashed.

I'm not joking.

I might try it again sometime. On paper.

Don't be put off by the complexity of these connections; it's better to look at them one time too many rather than one time too few.
Think about the handling of the horse, the schooling of both horse and rider, the tack and equipment, the keeping of the horse.

Everything can play a role in maintaining the health and well-being of the horse.

Even the really small things.

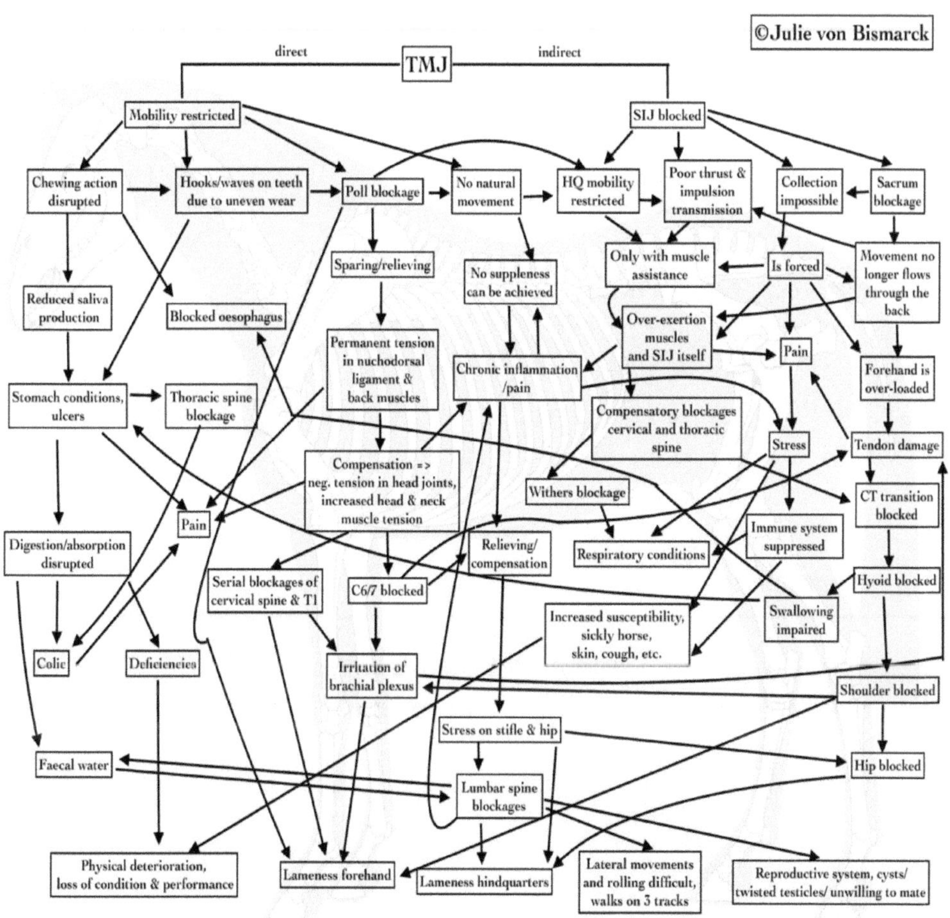
©Julie von Bismarck
direct
TMJ
indirect
Mobility restricted
SIJ blocked
Chewing action disrupted
Hooks/waves on teeth due to uneven wear
Poll blockage
No natural movement
HQ mobility restricted
Poor thrust & impulsion transmission
Collection impossible
Sacrum blockage
Reduced saliva production
Blocked oesophagus
Sparing/relieving
No suppleness can be achieved
Only with muscle assistance
Is forced
Movement no longer flows through the back
Stomach conditions, ulcers
Thoracic spine blockage
Permanent tension in nuchodorsal ligament & back muscles
Chronic inflammation /pain
Over-exertion muscles and SIJ itself
Pain
Forehand is over-loaded
Pain
Compensation => neg. tension in head joints, increased head & neck muscle tension
Compensatory blockages cervical and thoracic spine
Stress
Tendon damage
Digestion/absorption disrupted
Withers blockage
Relieving/ compensation
Respiratory conditions
Immune system suppressed
CT transition blocked
Serial blockages of cervical spine & T1
C6/7 blocked
Swallowing impaired
Hyoid blocked
Colic
Deficiencies
Irritation of brachial plexus
Increased susceptibility, sickly horse, skin, cough, etc.
Shoulder blocked
Faecal water
Stress on stifle & hip
Hip blocked
Lumbar spine blockages
Physical deterioration, loss of condition & performance
Lameness forehand
Lameness hindquarters
Lateral movements and rolling difficult, walks on 3 tracks
Reproductive system, cysts/ twisted testicles/ unwilling to mate

More books by Julie von Bismarck:

Zusammenhänge im Pferd Teil II
Connections in the horse part II

Mit dem Pferd statt auf dem Pferd - Ein Leitfaden für feines Reiten
With the horse not on the horse — a guide to fine riding

Reitsport - Auf dem Rücken des Pferdes
Equestrian sport — on the horse´s back

Reeva und die Pferde - Sommer auf Gut Balmore
Reeva and the horses — summer on Balmore estate

I would like to thank all the horses I have met in my life, who have taught me all that I know and still are teaching me new things every day.